Homeschooling

on the Cheap

By
Suzanne Stewart

Homeschooling on the Cheap
© 2010
ISBN 978 – 1 - 456 – 30147 - 7

All artwork is courtesy of Karen's Whimsy, and is either domain-free, or under purchased license.

This book is dedicated to my three favorite teachers,
My mother,
My daughter,
And
My son.

Table of Contents

Introduction - 11
Language Arts - 23
Maths – 67
Social Studies – 89
Science and Nature - 115
Art and Music - 131
Appendix - 147

Introduction

Hello There!

Who IS This Lady?

In the introduction of one of his books, the great Christian author C. S Lewis writes, "as one amateur to another, talking about the difficulties I have met, or lights I have gained…..with the hope that this might at any rate interest and sometimes even help, other inexpert readers." With this book, I feel very much the same way. I'm no expert homeschooler. I suppose the only experts are the ones no longer doing it because their children have all "graduated" and are now living successful, productive lives. I'm not one of those. I'm still in the trenches, right alongside you. I am a veteran of those trenches, though, and like Lewis hope that what I've learned may interest, and perhaps even help, other amateurs like me. So, think on me not as an expert touting wisdom from on high, but as a friend, offering advice over a cup of tea and a plate of cream scones.

Any and every good friendship starts with an introduction, a "*Hello. How are you? Nice to have you here!*" moment when two strangers cease to become unknown to one another. I suppose, therefore, that we should start the same way. I am a fellow homeschooling mom, down in the trenches right beside you, fighting the same battles, surviving the same struggles, and generally trying to keep my feet dry from one day to the next.

I've been homeschooling since 2002. Before marriage and children, I was a pre-Kindergarten/kindergarten teacher for three years. So when my daughter showed precociousness with language by recognizing certain words and letters by her third birthday, I thought, "Why not?" We began preschool homeschooling when she turned 4. I never really intended to *home school* home school, if you know what I mean, not past that first year anyway. Several things, however, conspired against me, and all my good intentions were for naught, as they say.

First, under the regulations of the time, my daughter's birthday fell 30 days after the last date for entry into Kindergarten. It would be another year before she would be allowed to attend public school anyway.

Secondly, by the end of that first year, she was reading at a first grade level and had completed an entire pre-kindergarten curriculum. I suppose we could've stopped there, but I really couldn't see a reason for doing so. She was eager to learn, more than capable of doing so, and was going to be home with me all day, every day anyway. Why not continue? Onward and upward we went!

Lastly, the more I became knowledgeable of the reasons for homeschooling, the more against the public education system I was once a part of I became. The schools were not the places of learning and inspiration they had been when I was a child. Safety and security weren't what they needed to be. Educational standards were far from what they had been, or should be. Character and morals teaching were practically non-existent. Discipline was either too lax or completely intolerant.

I began to yearn for a better way for my two children. I like to say that if you can name a reason to home school, it's already on my list of reasons somewhere, too. In fact, my usual response when asked why I choose to home school is a rather flippant "Pick one." Safer? You bet! More academically sound? Yep! Better able to meet my children's special needs? Oh yeah! More capable of instilling positive traits and behaviors in my children? Yes, sir! And so on and so on and so on………

So you see I became a dedicated homeschooler more or less by default. It hasn't always been a smooth journey, as few of Life's travels seldom are. I've made mistakes. I've pushed when I should've been more gentle and understanding. I've been gentle when I should've pushed and demanded a bit more. I've followed advice that I would've been better off ignoring. (Not that it was bad advice. It just wasn't the advice we needed at the time.) Like wise, I've put off doing some things that I now wish I hadn't. What did I tell you? I'm really not the *expert*. I have learned a great deal from my mistakes and shortcomings, though, and wish to save others from earning that same degree from the school of hard knocks.

Why Home School on the Cheap?

One thing I've always had to do was home school "on the cheap." I've never had the kind of money I would like to have to invest in our homeschooling venture. In the best spirit of the Great Depression, I've had to "make do or do without." For a while, at the beginning, I saw it as a handicap, a hindrance, even an insurmountable problem. Then, as time went on and I realized that my children were receiving a fairly fine education in spite of not having this fancy curriculum or that expensive program, I began to see that all my curriculum coveting was really not worth the time and effort I put into it. Why pine away for something I can't afford and obviously don't need? Why fret over this or that when my children are loving what we are doing, and better still, are thriving on it? I began collecting lists of free resources, utilizing methods that didn't require expensive purchases, and discovering alternatives to the pricey items I had once craved. As I had become a homeschooler by default, without prior planning or intention, so too did I fall into homeschooling on the cheap. I made it happen because I really had no other choice.

What DO You Do?

Good question. How to put a label or name on it? You might call me eclectic, but that really doesn't do me justice. I rely somewhat on the philosophies of Charlotte Mason and Ruth Beechick, but I'm not a strict Charlotte Mason devotee, nor do I follow every bit of Ms. Beechick's advice. I use a great deal of "classic" literature in our schooling, and while we do begin Latin instruction at age 11 and "cycle" our history study, we're not classical educators in the pure sense, either. My children, especially my son, love hands-on learning and exploration/discovery learning, but we're nowhere near to having a Montessori style atmosphere. We use unit studies and work in subject "blocks" sometimes, but ours is not a Waldorf school, either. We are who we are. We do what we do. And we do it without textbooks or expensive programs or pricey educational "toys." We use real literature, Real Life and the real world around us. In the process, we gain a living education. So, if you have to put a label on us, we're *living* educators. Education in our home is more than just something that happens for a few hours everyday. It's a lifestyle.

Those things and philosophies that we don't embrace were carefully considered and researched before being cast aside. Perhaps they wouldn't have worked for us, with our individual needs and talents. They may have been tried and found lacking or wanting in some way. They may not have been a better substitute for something that we were already engaged in. (Why fix it if it ain't broke?) In my search to do away with expensive, ineffective textbooks and traditional methods of teaching, I've done a great deal of research, of experimentation, and of soul searching. Our nearly text-book-free way of homeschooling has come about over a long 8 year process. I'm still not sure we've reached the end of the road. I've gained a lot of insight and inspiration from others over the years. I've read and studied, borrowed and copied from so many others in my quest to do what I do better – for myself and for my children. This book is my effort at giving some of that back, and in paying it forward to future travelers.

Why Write This Book?

One thing I often hear from non-homeschoolers is that they'd loved to "do it" but that it's "just too expensive." Even more frequently, I hear wails of despair from fellow veteran homeschoolers that they bought this or that and "it isn't working for us." They want to give "it" up but they can't because they "don't have the money" for something else. Worse yet, many feel obligated to continue soldiering bravely on simply because they spent so much on a costly program that isn't really what they needed or expected it to be. And then there are those who think to teach phonics or science or history or multiplication, they *have* to purchase this or that or the other thing, and the price just keeps climbing and climbing, while their children keep floundering and flailing. It is for those misinformed "newbies" and those struggling fellow veterans that *Homeschooling on the Cheap* was written. Anyone who has known me for very long will recognize much of the content in this book as the same old stuff I've said and practiced over and over (and over and over) again. Most of this book then is the same advice I've been giving newbies and old friends alike. For those readers who haven't had the pleasure of an introduction before now you'll hopefully glean some bit of insight or trick of my trade to prevent you from committing some costly mistake. To those new to homeschooling or are in the consideration stage, I hope you will see that not only *can* you afford to home school, when given the option, you really can't afford *not* to home school. To veteran homeschoolers, you'll recognize my ways are a combination of tried and true methods that, when combined as I have done, result in a very effective, fairly inexpensive way to teach your children. Is my way the only way to teach effectively and inexpensively? No, of course not. I'm not vain enough to think so. As with all things, take away what you will from what I say and do, and leave the rest for another day, another reading, or another reader. Just promise me you'll read with an open mind, and if something strikes a chord, don't ignore it. It's those small sparks that result in great blazes.

Can you REALLY Home School on the Cheap?

Sure. There is a trade off, though. Homeschooling on the cheap may not cost much in terms of money, but it does take *time.* Now, I don't mean it takes us very long to *do* our lessons every day – perhaps even less time than some curricula out there. But it does take a bit of planning and preparation. There's no teacher's manual or prepared lesson plans for you to consult. This is one of the biggest hurdles text-book addicts face when beginning to use living education methods. After a while, you get it down to an art or a science or whatever you want to call it, but I've never had anyone tell me they were still struggling to plan after using living education methods for a few months.

The biggest help I've found is my scope and sequence. By using it as a guide, I can plan my children's education in a logical, easy to follow manner. *So, they need to have learned about this or that by age 8? Alright, then let's plan a study on it. Oh, they don't have to know thus-and-such before moving on? Great! Let's forget it for now.* I can use my scope and sequence as a reference point for the entire year, then for each term or month, then for each week. For the year, I simply write out the broad terms, subjects, and concepts I'll need to cover. Then, I can break those down into units or blocks and create goals for each month and/or term. Lastly, I can look at my monthly goals and plan my weekly units. *February Language Arts – quotation marks and writing dialogue. Alright, let's find some good examples of dialogue and quotations for studying. September Maths – Geometry. Let's see, where did I put those Sir Cumference books again?* And because my scope and sequence is not by grade, or even by individual year, I don't have to worry if I don't cover something this year in favor of some other topic my children have taken an interest in. We can always get to it next year, instead. There isn't such a thing as "behind" with a living education. Your children are moving at their own pace, at the pace of their lives, not at the pace of some teacher's manual. Living education is all about life – it uses Real Life, and it transforms lives, both your children's and your own.

What Do I Need to Make This Work?

The biggest part of a living education is living books – real books, not textbooks, though you'll see there are a few places for a few of those here. So, you'll need a good library – either public or home – to provide you with the books you'll use as the basis of most of your learning. (You'll even find a place for living books in math lessons.) Now, a home library is something that can grow over time. Purchase a few basic resource books to start, and then build up from there. If you haven't got a decent public library or handy library system – don't forget the InterLibrary loan program if your library doesn't have what you need – you'll need to plan ahead and purchase accordingly. Something I've done is give family members our "upcoming" book list as ideas for holiday and birthday gifts – not the children's, mine!

As mentioned already, you'll need time. Time to plan, time to prepare, and time to research the library catalog or the book store shelves for what you need to do what you want. Once you become a parent, your time is no longer truly your own, as it belongs to your children. Once you become a homeschooling parent, you take on even more roles – teacher, principal, board of education, curriculum administrator – that will naturally take more of your time. For the veterans out there, this comes as no surprise, but for the newbies in the crowd, it can seem daunting at first. Just realize that several things will happen over time:

1.) Planning, teaching, preparing, shopping - it will all get easier as you become more practiced at it.
2.) Some things will just flow naturally from one thing to the next. Cursive typically follows manuscript, regardless of style of handwriting chosen, for example. The next thing may just be obvious.
3.) Your children and their abilities will often force the issue. He either is or isn't ready to read that novel. She either can or can't

play that level of music. Sometimes, you need to pause where you are and spend a while before moving on. That's alright. Those pauses often make the next thing easier to accomplish.
4.) A sense of adventure. You have look on this journey as the great adventure it is. Your children will be making discoveries nearly everyday, and so too will you. I can't tell you how excited homeschool parents can become because they've just found the *perfect* thing they've been searching for to teach their children maths or history or handwriting or whatever this week's/month's/term's/year's struggle has been.

C. S. Lewis also said, "The great thing, if one can, is to stop regarding all the unpleasant things as interruptions of one's "own," or "real" life. The truth is of course that what one calls the interruptions are precisely one's real life." Homeschooling on the cheap requires an open mind - to all the possibilities for learning that surround you every day. Remember, a living education relies on Real Life, takes place in Real Life, and is a part of Real Life. So, use what you're living, where you're living, as you're living it. Don't regard those interruptions as unpleasant. Use them for all they're worth! New baby in the house? Great opportunities for learning human development, good hygiene, sleep habits, nutrition, even telling time. *If the baby normally sleeps two hours between feedings, when will she most likely wake up?* Moving? Wonderful time to discuss time, distance, money, geography, even spatial reasoning skills. *How many toys will fit in this box?* Real Life doesn't stop for the interruptions, and neither should your living education.

About This Book

What You'll Find

Before we start, let me explain a bit about this book itself. The first, and main part of it, is made up of five chapters, covering Language Arts, Maths, Social Studies, Science, and the Arts. Each chapter is divided into sections, and the sections will be set off as they have been so far, with bold italics subtitles. I know that some of you may be looking for help or ideas in only one area of your teaching, and I've tried to accommodate those "skimmers" to the best that I am able.

Here's a brief look at what's ahead:

Language Arts – Ideas on how to endow your children with the greatest gift – literacy – using *real* books. I use literature, poetry, word games (I'll teach you a few) and working with language in *Real Life* to teach my children to read and write. You can, too, using little more than pencil, paper, dictionary, thesaurus and a library card. Come on, be Word Nerds like us!

Mathematics – Leave your days as a Maths Wimp behind! Make maths fun and fret-free with games, story books, manipulatives, puzzles and *Real Life*, with nary a workbook in sight.

Social Studies – Make the past come alive, travel to far away places and prepare your children to be responsible, informed future citizens by utilizing literature, atlases, globes and maps, and a timeline. It really can be that simple!

Science – Explore the wide world around you and inside you in the same manner as Galileo, da Vinci and Newton – by observing and *doing*, not by reading and filling in the blanks. You'll also find a list of the fun and exciting stuff that kids love to do, and should not be kept from doing.

The Arts – (Well, really only art and music.) Expose your children to great artists and famous composers and their masterpieces, even if you can't tell a Monet from a Mozart. Exercise your own artistic talents and create your own masterpieces along the way, too.

The Appendix – The various sections of the Appendix are full of resources to help you use the information in the book to the fullest extent possible. You'll find forms to help spark your little poets. You'll want to check out the list of literary maths titles. (Yes, there is such a thing.) The artist/composer timeline places prominent masters side by side with their contemporaries. The timeline template will aid in creating your own timeline notebooks.

Then, there's the scope and sequence. It's likely you've never seen one quite like its kind before. Without it, though, our home school is a traveler without a compass or map – lost and probably going in circles. I've included it to assist you in planning your own homeschooling journey. Instead of being separated into specific ages or grades, it has broader categories covering multiple ages, sometimes overlapping. Look on it as more of a guide – *By the time my child is 8 (or 10 or 14) she should have learned (or practiced or at least been introduced to) this and this and that.* Every child is different. Not every 8 year old is reading independently, while not every 10 year old is ready for fractions in math. Using traditional scope and sequence charts, mostly designed for classroom teachers, can often leave homeschoolers feeling inadequate or uncertain about where to go next. My scope and sequence was created out of my own frustrations with those traditional "one size fits all" classroom charts. It fits better into Real Life and our living education methods. Hopefully, it can serve you as well.

What You Won't Find

Alright, here's what you won't find here. With the exception of the literary maths books, there are no extensive booklists here. Throughout the book, I've listed the basic resource books that we've found invaluable in our homeschool. In a few places, I've given alternatives to what we've chosen, too. I only give these titles because I know they are worth the price, are quite useful, and using them as well might help you to better understand how it is we do what we do.

You won't find much mention of faith or religion here, either. I've tried to practice the Golden Rule throughout my life – treating everyone's beliefs as I would like to see mine treated, with respect and courtesy. I do mention *Christmas* a few times, but if you are Hindu, or Jewish or Muslim, you can replace the main religious and family celebration of our year with *Holi* or *Passover* or *Eid*, as suits your needs. I've tried to write a book that would appeal to *all* who might need it. I hope that I've succeeded.

You won't find much for preschoolers or high schoolers here, either. This book is mostly for those aged 4 to 14, the traditional elementary years. Why? Well, first of all there's the space. This book runs over 180 pages with the index now, just covering those ten years. Imagine its length had I tried to cover more! Secondly, the needs of preschool homeschoolers and high school homeschoolers are somewhat, if not vastly, different than those of elementary homeschoolers. It is my wish to write a book focusing on each of the other age groups in the future. If you are teaching high schoolers or preschoolers in your homeschool, many of the methods that I use and describe here will still work. Living books, hands-on activities, great art and music can all be used and enjoyed regardless of age, provided they are age and ability appropriate. Many of the resources and the nitty-gritty day-to-day stuff may not work so well for you, as your children will either be too old or too young to benefit from them fully.

Lastly, you won't find a bunch of edu-speak. Yes, I was a classroom teacher, but I never could remember all those educator's terms back then, and I haven't used them here. The scope and sequence is my best example of this. This book is as the first paragraphs described – the advice of a veteran homeschooler, from Real Life, in plain language. If you aren't American, you may find some of my spelling and word choices a bit funny, but you'll still find what I have to say pretty easy to understand. Oh, I suppose I should mention that this book isn't specifically American-oriented, either. I have friends in Australia, in Canada and in the UK who have read portions of this book and have said it would be quite worthwhile advice for their fellow homeschoolers, with the exception that some of the resources might need to be substituted for more available ones. So, I've tried to write this book with as broad an appeal and with as little confusion as possible. Hope you don't mind!

What's All This About FUN?

I'm often asked why the emphasis on "fun" in learning. Fun learning is easy to teach, because the student is open, receptive and excited about learning, and therefore more cooperative with the teacher. Fun learning is easier to learn, because the student isn't bored, pressured, or likely to "tune out" so the information or skill is remembered, retained and ready for future reference. Let me teach my children grammar through games, or math through a humorous story, or science through an exciting experiment any day. Fun learning is fulfilling learning. That's why all the "fun" in homeschooling on the cheap.

Conclusion

I would suggest that if you are new to the ideas of text-free teaching, you should read the book through once, completely, to get a general idea of what this exciting, wonderful way of learning and teaching is all about. Then, I'd suggest going back over it again, slower this time, to really understand just how to do the things we do. If you're only looking for ideas in one area or one subject, I'd still suggest you read the pertinent sections at least twice, making notes as you go, so you'll know for certain if what I have to offer is for you.

Hopefully, what you'll find is lots of friendly advice to kick the expensive homeschooling habit. You'll come across wonderful ways to make your learning enjoyable and fun. You'll stumble upon ideas on how to turn your ordinary days into extraordinary ones. You'll discover what it takes to be a Maths Wimp, why you don't want to be one, and how easy it is to become a Word Nerd. What you won't find is a lot of high pressure, high stress, high dollar homeschooling.

Whether you're the newest novice newbie, a possibly-someday window shopper kicking homeschooling's tires, or a war-weary old-timer looking for a better, more economical way to educate your children, or someone simply curious as to what this *Homeschooling on the Cheap* thing is all about, I invite you to settle yourself for a nice long chat. Pour yourself a cup. Have a scone. Make yourself comfortable. *Hello! How are you! It's so nice to have you here!*

∞ ∞ ∞

Language Arts

Introduction

It is no mistake that I chose language as the first subject to explore in depth in this book. Teach a person to read, and there is *nothing* he can't learn, discover and experience, on his own. Every previously shared thought, declaration and deed, every adventure, every tragedy, every triumph – real or imagined – is his for the taking by simply reading about it. Teach a person to write and there is *nothing* he learns, discovers, and experiences, on his own, that can't be shared with others. His every thought, declaration and deed, every adventure, every tragedy, every triumph – real or imagined – is his for the sharing by simply putting it into words. Teach a child to read and you open up the world to him. Teach a child to write and you open him up to the world.

Language skills are also, by their very importance, some of a homeschooling parent's worst nightmares. *What if he never learns to read? Why can't she write a decent sentence? What am I to do with all their spelling mistakes?* And what drives our fears drives us to turn to others. We can't possibly teach these all-important language skills without expert help, and it better be the best, the most expensive, the latest-greatest, all the bells and whistles help, too. Right? Well, not exactly. That's another reason why I've chosen language arts as my first subject to homeschool on the cheap. Because it can be done – very simply, effectively and inexpensively.

Sadly, many parents only find this out after purchasing some pricey comprehensive "boxed" program. Oh, they're nice programs all right. Everything is right there, all laid out for you with lesson plans and schedules and scripts and well, everything. All the subjects are integrated so that each skill is practiced across the board. This week's spelling and vocabulary words come from this week's stories in the leveled readers, while also serving as the content of this week's handwriting practice. Meanwhile, grammar instruction uses examples from the readers to illustrate this week's concepts. Everything is tickety-boo-perfect until Real Life steps in and suddenly you have chaos on your hands. Your child has declared the lovely readers to be stupid, boring and dumb, which they probably are if you stop and really read one of them. Your second grader isn't quite physically ready to transition from manuscript to cursive handwriting just yet. (Many, especially boys, take longer to develop those fine motor skills.) Your fourth grader isn't reading fluently enough to handle all that the program requires. (There is a huge jump between 3rd and 4th grade in many programs in terms of independent work and ability required.) Your third grader can't remember what a noun is to save her life, yet the next twenty integrated grammar lessons on adjectives and pronouns are all counting on her having mastered that crucial bit of knowledge. (I've personally experienced this with my own children.) Let's not forget that the phonics program brings your five year old to tears every time you bring it off the shelf. Your pricey program isn't working anymore. At least not for you.

Then there are the parents who attempt to save a little money by cobbling together their own program to teach language arts skills from bits and pieces of other curricula. *Phonics book? Check! Readers? Check! Handwriting book? Check! Grammar book? Check! Composition program? Check! Oooops! Almost forgot about spelling. Check! Literature and poetry – ummm, isn't that covered in the reader?!?* What they end up with is usually a rather hefty check filled out to one or more curriculum sellers, along with a conglomeration of products that make skill integration difficult, if not impossible. The speller's lesson 3 includes a phonetic blend not introduced until the readers' 26th lesson, while the grammar book asks the child to write several sentences incorporating proper use of capital letters that your handwriting book hasn't gotten around to teaching yet. Again, Real Life dictates another round of the dreaded Curriculum Chaos Crazies. So, before you start perusing the catalogs in search of the next big thing that will be the magic bullet that solves all your problems and turns all your children into future Pulitzer Prize winners, let's explore how to teach language arts on the cheap.

Technically, all you really need to teach language skills is paper, pencil and something to read. After all, Abraham Lincoln had less than that and somehow accomplished literacy. I know of no one, however, in today's world, who gets by with so little. For one thing, most homeschoolers, myself included, like to have some sort of scope and sequence, especially for something as important as language skills, to ensure that we leave no gaps in our children's education. For another, given the choice of using something someone else has done for us and that others have proven to work, why reinvent the wheel? Lastly, few of us really have the time and energy to devote to reinventing that wheel. So a few wise choices, a few tricks of the trade and a few tried and true techniques can provide you and your children with more than sufficient language arts learning.

Before going on with specifics, I'd like to add a note concerning the importance of mastery of basic skills in language arts learning. I'd rather see a child form each letter effortlessly and legibly after a year of practice, than to rush her through a handwriting course so she "doesn't get behind the other kids" and have her come out on the other side with horrid, barely readable handwriting. (I'm speaking from sad, sorry experience here.) The phonics book may swear that after 95 daily lessons the child will be ready to read Dr. Seuss. If he misses a key element in le4sson 42, however, that causes difficulties with every lesson after that, wouldn't it be wiser to go back to lesson 42 and make sure he masters what he's missed instead of forging forward in the hopes that he "gets it" someday? Slow, steady progress is preferable over speedy finishes. Missteps and gaps in basic skills will cause no end of grief and headache later. Speeding through without assuring mastery will mean lengthier detours later, as remedial instruction takes the place of forward motion, and old, bad habits must be overcome and replaced with new learning. It's just not worth it in the end –in time, money or self-esteem.

Reading

The first step in language skills is reading. Fancy phonics programs for preschoolers and early elementary students abound. You don't need videos, computers, fancy toys or bells, whistles, beeps or boops, however. All you need is a little time, a little preparation and a few simple materials and you have everything you need to begin your journey to literacy.

Start with a letter a week. Cut it out of fancy paper (scrapbooking sheets and wallpaper samples are good for this) or print out a really snazzy version from your computer's font collection. Teach your child the letter's name and most common sounds. Paste that cut out or print out on a piece of cardstock. Cut out or print out photos or illustrations of objects that begin with that letter and make a collage or mini poster. Read story books that feature one or more of these objects. (Apples, Bears, Cats, Dogs, Elephants,

Frogs, etc. There's a list in the Appendix for you.) Teach your child tongue twisters that feature that letter and its sound. If your child is ready, write or paint or trace the letter. Put all these pages together and create your very own alphabet and beginning phonics book. Ours was in the shape of a house and each week's pages were another addition to Alphabet Town.

One your child has mastered the alphabet and initial phonetics, start using the sounds and putting them together. Take a couple of sets of index cards and make 3 or 4 sets of alphabet cards out of them. Play memory games where the child has to sound out the letters as her turns them over. See how many simple C-V-C (consonant-vowel-consonant *M – A – T. Mat. B – A – G. Bag. S – I – T. Sit*) words can be made out of a hand of 6 cards. Take one ending, like A-T, and find all of its initial consonants. Take the initial consonant and a vowel and see if you can build words with all of its ending consonants. Make sentences, silly or otherwise, with the words you make up and practice reading them. See who can make the longest or silliest sentences. Play these games every day until the child has mastered the short vowel sounds and initial consonants. Next, add the common beginning and ending "blends" - BR, GL, SH, TH, WH, CH, etc. (a complete list of these is in the Appendix.) You're slowly but carefully adding to your child's reading ability and reading vocabulary, in a fun and fairly painless way. If you need to, once you've added the blends, go back to the Memory games until the child has learned the blended sounds, then proceed on. Once again, play games of making and reading words, silly sentences, learning through simple card games. When you feel your child is ready, add silent E and the long vowel sounds. Then, add the variations that exist on the long vowel sounds (OU, OW, EA, EE, etc.) It might be best to stick with one long vowel sound, long E for example, through its various spellings, before moving on to another. Again, in this way, your child is learning, playing and reading all at the same time. By now, this method of playing games has become familiar to him. And so has reading, a great deal of reading if you stop and think about it. From the very beginning, you should read real books together, as well. Allow your child to read the words she knows or can sound out, while you read the rest of the unknown, unfamiliar words. You won't need to advance to lesson 95 before reading Dr. Seuss, and your child will have interesting, exciting stories for reading practice, not "dull, boring, stupid" leveled readers.

Sight words are words that the reader is expected to know and read instantly and automatically. Experts differ on the number of sight words, but the general consensus is that 60% to 70% of all reading is a combination of sight words, making the learning of sight words vital to all future reading success. You'll have to include those "irregular" words that don't fit or follow standard phonics rules, too. They can be taught in several ways. You can use the old tried and true flash card method. It can get boring, but for some children it does work best. You can make several sets of sight word cards and play Memory and Go Fish type games as you did (or are doing) with basic phonics. You can stop and point them out every time you encounter them in stories. You can teach them one or two or ten at a time, until the child is familiar with those and ready to move on to new words. You can use them to make word search, cross word or fill-in puzzles. I'd suggest doing it all, really. With so much of reading resting on the 300 to 500 sight words, I'd rather "over teach" them than play hit or miss with my child's reading abilities.

Reading, especially sight words, goes beyond mastery, by the way. Mastery implies that a child has learned the material well enough to be tested on it with a successful outcome – the child can score well on a test, or a thorough narration can be given, or the skill successfully displayed through completion of a project or task. Once mastered, though, a skill or concept can be forgotten, especially if repeated practice is not continued. With reading, we want our children to have reached automaticity. We want them to know what the word is without having to sound it out or think about it. We want them to reach a point where they can read the word as easily as they breathe, so that reading is quick and easy and enjoyable for them. Struggling readers often know their phonics, they've sometimes even "mastered" their sight words, but they've not reached the level where reading is automatic for them. If your child is struggling with reading, don't put it aside and don't put great amounts of money into it, either. Go back to the basics and play games, have fun and learn it over again, together. You'll be surprised how quickly a struggling reader can flourish when the pressure is off and the "fun" is on.

Comprehension

The other side of reading is comprehension. All the phonics and decoding skills and sight words in the world are of no use if your child can't understand what she's reading. You also have to determine if what is being read *to* your child is being understood. Most reading programs assess comprehension skills through quizzes, tests, worksheets or complete workbooks. Many times, though, these methods can only test for certain levels or types of comprehension, leaving things like inference or analysis to upper levels, even though younger students are quite capable of comprehending and relating to their readings on various levels.

So, the most effective way to test your child's comprehension of her readings is by taking a page from 19th century educator Charlotte Mason. She advocated the use of a technique called narration. Narration is nothing more than a re-telling – oral or written – of what the child has heard or read. It can be as simple as asking "What happened in our story today?" or as complex as some of the questions listed on the next two pages.

For young children, I advocate what I call "engaged" or active narration. Engaged narrating can take several forms:

- Acting out a scene from a story
- Drawing a character or setting or scene
- Sculpting a character or setting from clay or play dough
- Building the setting with blocks or dollhouse furniture
- Pretending the child is a television or radio news reporter giving an account of the story or scene on the air
- Imagining a character as a friend and describing him or her
- Writing a letter to someone, telling that person about the wonderful adventure from the story that the child went on with the story's characters

Younger children, aged 4 to 8 or 9, tend to do one of two things when giving standard oral narrations. They either become overwhelmed to the point they can't remember anything, or they give rambling on and on "and then" narrations. Using engaged narrations allows them to focus on the important elements of the reading, while giving them a place to start and a creative form of expression.

Older children, say ages 10 to 12 and up, can produce both oral and written narrations. The Narration Starters found below were taken from exam questions Charlotte Mason actually used in her PNEU schools in Britain. They are somewhat arranged by the complexity of thought needed to answer them, with the simplest listed first.

Narration Starters

To use these, you can either simply ask the child the question and receive an oral answer, or write/type the question out and have the child write her response.

1.) Tell what you remember about_____
2.) Tell me the story in your own words.
3.) Wasn't it funny/sad/strange when_____? Tell me what else you remember about that.
4.) Explain how _____happens/happened.
5.) Describe _____.
6.) Tell me who we met today. Describe him/her.
7.) Tell me all you can about (a particular setting.)
8.) Tell me all you can about (the reading's time period.)
9.) Tell me everything that happened after _____.
10.) Tell all you know about how _____ happens.
11.) Tell about a problem in the story and how it was solved/fixed.
12.) Tell everything you would see (in a particular setting.)
13.) Tell me all you know about (a particular character or person)
14.) Who said, "----------"? Tell me the story about it.
15.) Why did he/she do _____?"
16.) List the story's events in the order that they happened.
17.) Describe the clues that lead up to _____.
18.) From the passage/story we read, tell me how to _____.
19.) Tell me how he/she felt after _____
20.) Describe the narrator.
21.) Describe everything that happened because of_____
22.) Tell me all the ways two characters/people/settings from the same

story compare.

23.) Tell me all the ways two characters/people/settings from two different stories compare.

24.) Compare this book/story to another of the same style.

25.) Compare this book/story to another by the same author.

26.) Explain how _____ came to be.

27.) Did he/she make the right decision? Tell me why or why not.

28.) Tell me all you know about (time period/character traits/sequence of events.) [This involves a higher level of thinking than the earlier questions similar in nature. The information you are asking for here is to be implied or inferred, not directly stated in the reading. In other words, I might ask, "Tell me all you know about what is happening before the story begins" or "Tell me all you know about Aunt Lucy" even though in the story the only time we "meet" Aunt Lucy is through her letters to the main character.)

29.) Who/what had the most influence on the outcome of the story? Why? How?

30.) Would you want him/her as a friend? Why or why not?

When discussing narration, it should be noted that no two individuals will ever give the same narration, as no two people will ever remember the same story in the same way. What we recall from a reading depends on so many different factors – from distraction levels to personality traits – that we all latch on to different aspects and let others slide right on by. Don't be surprised then, if one child remembers a piece of dialogue word for word while another child can't even recall the conversation having taken place! Because of this, some parents find it difficult to judge whether a child has retained enough pertinent facts to have a true comprehension of the reading. Some will argue that if a child can't retell *all* the major events or points or facts from the reading, then she hasn't really understood it. I prefer to determine comprehension by the three-to-five-finger rule. If my children can tell me three to five things relevant to the reading, then they've understood and attended to the reading closely enough for my satisfaction.

Don't restrict narrations simply to fiction stories. Looking over the 30 Narration Starters, you'll see questions that could be used for a number of non-fiction subjects. Number 12 could prove useful after historical or geographical readings, for example, while #18 would be quite appropriate for science or math selections. Number One is indeed the all-purpose Mother-of-All-Narration-Starters. You could ask it after reading a biography, a geography, a science article, a how-to manual, a recipe or a picture book. Your children's readings aren't limited. Neither should be your desire to check their understanding through narrations.

How often should narrations be done? Charlotte Mason devotees will tell you the child should provide some sort of narration after every reading. I disagree. I like the rule of thumb of two or so a day. Asking for narration after every reading becomes tedious for both teacher and child, in our experience. Two or 3 narrations a day are enough to gauge attention and comprehension without taxing everyone's patience.

Remember to keep your readings short, especially for younger children. I don't read, nor do I require my children to read, more than one chapter from any one title per day. Most chapters can be read in 10 to 20 minutes, keeping young minds focused and fresh for the task of attending to the reading. Expecting attention and retention after that is asking a bit much, in my opinion. As a child ages and matures, reading times of 30 and even 45 minutes can be attained. Start slow. Start small. It'll be better for all.

Handwriting

After teaching a child to read, the next basic skill to learn is handwriting. If your child is physically ready and able, you can teach letter formation alongside letter recognition. If he is not ready, it's better to wait and develop those fine motor skills fully. Starting a child too soon leads to frustration, produces poor handwriting, and often results in bad habits that must be overcome later.

Copy work is the basis for all handwriting programs. The child is taught letter formation through tracing, and then is asked to reproduce the letter independently for so many lines. After letter formation is learned, the letters are used to create words and sentences which are again traced and then reproduced. You can create your own handwriting program using these same basic principles of copy work, whether teaching your 6 year old to print, or your 14 year old a fancy calligraphic script.

Purchase one of those primary tablets with the colored and dotted lines. Buy a purple highlighting pen, too. Familiarize yourself enough with the script or font you want to teach so that you can use it to create your copy work pages. Begin with the most meaningful thing any living person can see in print – his or her own name. Teach the letters of the first name. Then move on to the letters contained in the last name. Don't worry if some of the letters taught are repeats – repetition speeds mastery. Using your purple pen, write out several examples for your child to trace over. (This is why purple highlighting pens work best – they are dark enough to provide easily traceable lines, while light enough for the child's tracing to be easily visible.) Then, require 5 or 10 repetitions or reproductions.

Once the names are mastered, move on to other meaningful letters, such as those in your address or the names of other family members or pets. Use quotes, lines from poems or songs, Scripture verses, maxims, proverbs, whatever your child finds meaningful or interesting; to teach proper letter formation, spacing and word spacing. Remember – mastery of skill is the goal, not how many lines can be reproduced. To that end, keep to one-liners and 5 to 10 repetitions of that one line, to allow adequate, but not taxing, daily practice. Daily practice of one line of text will lead to mastery quicker than copying paragraphs or entire poems. When faced with long copy work selections, young hands and fingers tire, young attentions wander, and the handwriting produced is less than the best effort. Even young adults, learning calligraphy, appreciate short passages while learning. My rule of thumb for copy work is one line per year of practice. By this I mean that a child in their first year of learning *any* script – manuscript, italics, cursive, any form of calligraphy – should be given one line of copy work per day. Now, if you are reviewing or practicing a script already learned, say a 10 year old practicing neat manuscript learned at the age of 6, a longer passage is permissible.

Some say a child should learn some form of manuscript first, before any other handwriting. Others preach italics or cursive for the beginner. I don't think it really matters. Mastery is far more important than the style of writing taught or the age of the student upon beginning.

(Some lessons are learned the hard way! My daughter wasn't ready but I pushed her into handwriting anyway, because she was "old enough" to learn.

As a consequence, her cursive writing, taught when she was 8, was much more legible than her italics manuscript handwriting taught at 5 years old. When in fifth grade, at age 10, she asked to learn manuscript again the "right way this time," her printing greatly improved, and continues to do so.)

Composition

I disagree with Charlotte Mason advocates when it comes to teaching composition skills. They believe that children learn to write simply by reading and being read to from quality writing. I do agree that good literature exposure is important to the development of a child's overall language skills, and perhaps writing skills in particular, but I believe that a child learns to write best through writing his own compositions, modeling his work on the quality literature he has been read and is reading on his own. Writing is not something that comes natural to most, but modeling our work after that of others does. A baby learns to talk by modeling the sounds she hears spoken around her. A child learns table manners by modeling the examples he sees in the familial society around him. So, too, can a child learn to write by modeling the writing presented to him in good, quality literature selections.

Therefore, to begin composition instruction, you must begin by reading to your child. If you want to teach story formation, read classic stories. If you want your older child to learn to write thoughtful, persuasive essays, read essays together. If you want to teach a certain type of poetry, read several selections that exemplify that type of poem. If you want to teach descriptive writing, fables, myths, research reporting, or journalistic editorial writing, *read* it first. Stories come naturally to younger children because it is the type of writing they are most familiar with because we read and tell them stories. Poetry will come somewhat naturally, too, if it is made a part of daily or weekly readings. The better quality the reading selection, and the more varied types of reading selections we give our children, the better and more varied their own compositions will be. And that's pretty much where the Charlotte Mason-ites would stop. Read it and they will write. Ummmmm, sorry, but in my experience and in the experiences of many others, it doesn't always happen that way. There's more to it than that.

That something more is oral reproduction. More than a narration, oral reproduction asks the student to retell the story or poem or whatever in as closely the same manner and style as the original reading. You aren't just looking for a retelling of the main points of the reading, but also at how those main points were presented. This oral reproduction introduces the child to the rhythms and word choices, the meter, the tone and the style of the author. They become, even if just for a moment, a part of the child. Enough oral reproduction of any one particular author and those elements of his writing becomes the student's to use as she wishes, for she knows somewhat how to use them now.

Once the child has reached a place of comfort and ease with oral reproductions, help her to see and recreate that same invisible framework that makes up that particular kind of writing. Much more than a simple outline of the piece, this framework also includes the elements the student has already learned through oral reproduction – word choice, timing, rhythm, cadence, style, and all the other things that make a story a story, or a ballad a ballad, or a persuasive essay a persuasive essay. The framework for a fable is easy enough to follow – a story followed by a moral. The story itself is an example of the moral, and often uses talking animals or other fantastic components, to teach the moral's lesson. Ask a child who has heard many fairy tales to create a framework for one and she will almost inevitably begin, "Once upon a time…." and end with "and they all lived happily after." A haiku poem has a very strict framework of syllables per line, and nature as a subject. Even sentences have a basic subject-verb framework that must be adhered to in order to be considered complete sentences. Once a child can recognize the basic framework of the type of writing being studied, she can begin to create her own original writings.

To begin original compositions, start with the basic framework. Create outlines, or create reminder lists, so that the basic elements and essential components are not forgotten. Only after a child can create the basic framework should she be required to write the composition. She'll be much more comfortable doing so, because she knows what to include, and what is expected of her as a writer. Simply asking a child to "Write a story" without giving her the basics of reading, reproducing, and framing beforehand is sort of like asking you to drive a car without showing you where the key goes in.

Read, reproduce, frame, and then write. It's a sure way to defeat reluctant writers, writer's block and poorly prepared writers.

Don't forget to urge your children to create interesting writing. Often, a child's limited vocabulary, or spelling ability, or reading ability, leads to limited word choices in their writing and to stories with sentences of all the same length. Defeat this through proper preparation of your young writer's mind. We play a game called "Sentences." Start small, with a two word sentence. Then, we each have to add another word to the sentence. Then another word, and another, going round the table adding words until the sentence is about as complex as we can make it. Then we do it again, with another 2 word sentence. And again. And again. When we're at home, we often write them out, watching our sentence grow as we play. But this is also the perfect game for in the car, or while washing dishes together, or while standing in line at the market. Do this often enough and your children will seldom produce boring lifeless writing because they'll know what makes sentences interesting expressions of what they have to say, even if they can't spell half the words.

Creative Writing

The difference between creative writing (or free writing) and composition is that creative writing is an exercise in self-expression and composition is an exercise in skill or technique. You can use composition as part of your creative writing program, but doing it the other way round tends to squash some creativity, especially in young and reluctant writers. "Read a story. Outline a story. Now write a story." Just sounds creativity sapping, doesn't it?

Some children are natural "word nerds." I was one, and my daughter has word nerd tendencies. We word nerds can be recognized by our love of putting words to paper. We scribble poems and stories from the time we can hold the pencil or pen properly. For word nerds, a journal to fill with stories, responses to journaling "prompts," descriptions of our daily lives, or poems plucked from the recesses of our word nerdy minds is heaven on earth.

Some children, however, seem to suffer from near-terminal page fright. Faced with a blank piece of paper and a potential writing assignment, they'd gladly clean their rooms, their younger sister's room, the garage, the attic *and* empty every trash bin in the neighborhood first. How to engage such reluctant writers? As with everything else – start slow, start small, and build gradually. They may never really enjoy writing, but they will learn that it isn't the worst thing they can be asked to do, either.

I have three techniques that keep both my word nerd daughter and my page frightened son inspired and writing. The first is a journal with prompts. The second are poetry forms. Lastly, I have my arsenal of Roll-a-Tale charts.

Journals

Many, many sources for kids' journaling prompts exist, from free lists on the Internet, to pre-printed journals with a prompt per page. I've found many, if not most, of these are inappropriate for homeschoolers because they are geared toward classroom dwellers. Their prompts cover topics from "Who is your favorite teacher?" to "What's your favorite food in the cafeteria?" to "What is your favorite way to spend your school holidays?" (Many of their other prompts are so bland and boring that I can't see how they inspire *any* child to write, really.) As with any learning, personal relevance to the learner goes much farther towards engaging the student than bland generics. Therefore, if you expect journaling prompts to actually *prompt* your child to write, they need to be personal, relevant, and interesting to him. If that means that your child is writing about animals, or Star Wars characters, or knights and dragons, then so be it. He's writing, and isn't that the whole point of the thing? You know your child and her interests best – you can create your own prompts for inspiring your young writer quickly and easily if you give it a try.

Journaling should not take only one form, either. No one really wants to write a paragraph or a page every day, day in and day out. There are all sorts of other writing that can qualify for a journal entry. Here's a not-so-short list:

- Newspaper report
- Advertisement
- Limerick
- Haiku
- 30 second radio ad
- Song lyric

- Riddle
- Palindrome
- How-to instructions
- Campaign speech
- Dialogue
- Diamonte poem
- Concrete poem
- Word pyramid
- List of adjectives
- Fable
- Moral
- Play script
- Letter
- Complaint

By providing prompts that your child finds interesting and a wide choice of possibilities for the final written product, you're almost assured to receive something more than the one or two sentences your page frightened student has been producing. You'll almost eliminate the tears, fears, fussing and fuming normally associated with writing assignments in the past. Limiting journal entries to 1 to 3 a week to start will also allow the new or reluctant writer to slowly build confidence, skill and hopefully, a liking for producing the written word.

Poetry Forms

Poetry forms take two formats. The first is similar to a worksheet. The student is given lines to finish, such as an "I am" poem or a Biography poem (I was born……I live……..I like to…….) and acrostic poetry, where the student is given the letters of the subject word down the page, and is asked to write a word or line that begins with that letter and centers on that subject somehow. The second type of form is an outline or reminder, of what is required by certain types of poems. These are for poems that *must* follow certain guidelines such as haiku, diamonte poetry, senryku, sonnets, and limericks. The student doesn't write on these – she uses these to guide her own poetry. In fact, my children don't write on any of our poetry forms. They simply use pencil or pen and paper, copying anything from the worksheet type form while writing. (You can find a few of my poetry forms in the Appendix.) Word nerds find both types of forms fun and challenging, while page-frightened pups find them less intimidating than a blank piece of paper and the assignment to "write a poem." My own page frightened son is often surprised by the fact that he has actually written a *gasp* poem while using one of our poetry forms!

Roll-a-Tale

The idea for our Roll-a-Tale charts came from a British teacher. I've adapted it from his four charts to our three, and also changed many of the original ideas he had included in his charts to make them better suit my American, homeschooled children. The creative reader will probably adapt *my* charts to better meet the needs in her homeschool, too. I include my charts here to serve as an inspiration, and so you can have a visual to aid in understanding what I'm talking about.

You'll need at least 1 die (2 are better) and the three charts. Roll the die or dice. The first number decides the column. The second number rolled (or the second die) determines the row. Find that box and you've got your setting, main character, or plot problem. Repeat the process with the other two charts and you're all set to write. For example a roll of 4 and 3 will result in a setting of a parade for a story. Roll-a-Tale is sure to produce some outlandish combinations. It is those very outrageous combos of character, setting and plot possibilities that make using the activity exciting and engaging for reluctant writers. Word nerds find Roll-a-Tales present them with creative opportunities even they hadn't thought of yet!

Settings Chart

Zoo	Park	Fair	At the lake	Back Yard	Your house
Spaceship	Wedding	Amusement Park	In the desert	In the woods	A cloud
Circus	Grandma's house	On a ship	At a Parade	In a tree house	A flower
Birthday Party	On Mars	By the river	Sporting event	Farm	Underground
Castle	Hospital	Mountains	Restaurant	The Jungle	An Island
Museum	Beach	North Pole	South Pole	A Cave	Art Gallery

Character Chart

Clown	Pirate	Robot	Kitten	Fairy	Boy/Girl
Puppy	Prince/Princess	Fish	Flower	Mouse	Dancer
Movie Star	King/Queen	Football player	Police Officer	Knight	Horse
Bird	Butterfly	Spider	Raindrop	Chocolate Bar	Farmer
Doctor	Fire Fighter	Superhero	Frog	Tree	Teddy Bear
Doll	Car	Alien	Monster	House	Snowflake

Plot Problem Chart

Looking exactly like someone else	Tracking down a thief	Losing your memory	Becoming very tiny	Becoming very large	Finding buried treasure
A runaway train	Trapped on a sinking ship	Taking a bath	A strange shining light	The last train home	Only two more days to live
A genie's visit	A door to another time	Lost in a thick fog	Someone calling for help	Pictures that come to life	Animals that suddenly know how to speak
Face to face with a mummy	Turned into another creature	Suddenly a millionaire	Vanished!	Escaped!	Stolen!
Alien invasion	Thrown into a dungeon	Battling a hurricane	Pirates!	Shark!	Pigeons!
Growing wings	Becoming a mermaid	Becoming a movie star	Lights!	Camera!	Action!

The 9 plot problems that end in an exclamation point are left up to the child's imagination. Perhaps Pirates! Is a good thing, not bad. Perhaps Lights! Means a movie is being made, or there are suddenly strange lights in the sky, or it's what someone calls out because the house suddenly goes dark. It was a way to give the writer just a little more freedom to maneuver within the context of the chart activity.

Once you've taught an aspect of composition, it will only be natural to see that element pop up in your children's creative writings. Assigning a child some sort of exercise or composition to "test" for that skill isn't really "creative" writing, though. That's why I make a distinction between composition and creative writing. Composition exercises should be used to teach and practice the skills needed to become a good writer. Creative writing exercises should be used to have fun with the written language and to stretch imagination and creativity muscles. Think of composition exercises as the blueprints an architect makes in preparation for his building project. They are creative in nature, but technical in purpose and design. Creative writing exercises, then, can be seen as the artist's rendition or scale model of the architect's finished project – creative in vision and purpose. The better the blueprint, the better the model or sketch, but one requires much more attention to technical details, while the other relies on creative interpretation of those details. Composition exercises can help our children build better creative writing, but one without the other, or a substitution of one for the other, doesn't create the well-rounded writers we want our children to become.

Spelling

When it comes to spelling, there are three methods that are both effective and inexpensive. You can teach using dictation, using your children's own misspelled words, or by using word families. All have their merits, and are highly superior to traditional spelling programs.

Traditional programs tend to follow one of two routes, or a combination of both. They either teach using phonetic rules – all the words in this week's list contain some from of long E, or exemplify the two sounds of G, for example. These programs work great if your child is capable of reading all the words on each week's list. Or they teach the spelling "rules" – all of this week's words have an I before E, or are all plurals using –ES. These programs work wonderfully if your child is able to transfer what he's learned in spelling to other words with similar pronunciations. If your child isn't a strong enough reader, or has difficulty relating spelling rules to writing on his own, then all the wonderful programs in the world won't improve his spelling abilities.

Dictation

Using dictation is possibly the simplest and easiest way to teach spelling. You simply choose a passage, have the child study the passage for a few days, and then the student writes the passage as you dictate it. This form of so-called "studied" dictation allows you to choose passages that are interesting and relevant to the student, while being an example of words or sounds or spelling rules (or combinations of all of them) that you'd like your child to learn. Instead of lists of words, the words are presented in their "natural" setting, in sentences, stanzas and paragraphs. Instead of one phonetic rule or one spelling rule, a whole host is present. Instead of limiting words to grade level or reading ability, a mix of words known and unknown can be taught, so that the student is constantly expanding and developing her vocabulary and spelling abilities.

A few rules of thumb for choosing and using dictation passages:

1. Dictation passages can come from anywhere – your read-aloud; a poem, Scripture verse, or song; your history text; a scientist's biography; the daily newspaper – in short, anything you are currently using in your lessons or anything you have at hand that has some interest or relevancy to the student.
2. Dictation passages should be age-appropriate in length. I like the rule of 1 sentence per every 2 years of age. So, a seven year old would be given 3 sentences. A ten or twelve year old could easily dictate a short paragraph or several stanzas of a poem.
3. Regardless of age, when first starting to use dictation in your language lessons, start slow and start small. Gradually increase the length and complexity of the passages until your child is challenged but not overwhelmed. Giving a 10 or 12 year old who has never done a dictation lesson before a 6 or 8 sentence paragraph may easily crush her confidence in her abilities to ever complete a dictation with any success.

4. When dictating to a child, read the passage slowly, a few words at a time, with no more than one repetition. Giving two or three words at a time is enough to keep the child working, without worrying about losing attention to what you are saying for the sake of concentrating on their writing. I only repeat any one portion once, though, to ensure that attentions don't wander off while I'm reading.
5. Dictation is useful for grammar lessons, too. This is explained in full next in the grammar section of this chapter.

Here's how dictation works at our house. On Monday, the passage is introduced. The student and I read it together, several times if necessary, until the child can read it by himself. I then do an initial dictation and any spelling errors are pointed out and corrected. Then, he has Tuesday, Wednesday, and Thursday to practice and study the passage. We do this by repeated readings and copying of the passage, usually two readings and one copy per day. Then, come Friday, he takes his dictation. His dictated passage is compared to the original and is marked accordingly. If there are a significant number of mistakes, then he repeats the passage the following week. If he has reproduced the passage with few or no mistakes, then the next week we move on to something different.

My children have found that dictation makes spelling fun and interesting, as it's never just a bunch of words in a list that is memorized for Friday's test and then forgotten as we move on. Dictation reinforces and reviews words they've already learned, too, effortlessly and easily, as they are repeated in passage after passage. Remember – 60 to 70% of all text is comprised of the same 300 to 500 words. So, it is only natural that dictation, using passages from various texts, will supply the student with plenty of practice with a large number of the same words, while introducing them to a large number of new words as well. It may seem like a daunting task, coming up with new passages every week. It's not really, though, as you are constantly presented with new ideas, new sources, for passages as you read and learn and travel through your homeschooling days.

Children's Misspellings

Some parents prefer to use their children's own misspellings as a source of spelling materials. After all, if their children can't properly spell certain words, those are the words they need to learn to spell, right? To do this, you have to have a steady source of writing to pick the words from, such as weekly journaling or written narrations or compositions. You simply keep a list of words that you add to after each week's writing is reviewed. Then, you use that list in much the same way as traditional spelling programs use their lists – by having the student perform some form of spelling exercise or practice. When we tried this method, I made up index cards with 10 different ideas for spelling practice written on them. I placed these in an envelope and each day, my children had to pull one card (without looking) from the envelope and do as instructed by the card. It kept their spelling practice fresh and somewhat fun, and was easy for me, as the cards took a half hour or so to create and then were used for the entire school year. Here are our ten spelling practices:

1. Alphabetize your spelling words.
2. Divide your words into two lists – those starting with consonants and those starting with vowels.
3. Divide your spelling words into two lists – plural and singular words. If you can, write the plural form of all singular words, and the singular form of all plural words.
4. Write your spelling words from longest to shortest.
5. Divide your words into lists by their number of syllables.
6. Underline any similar word parts – prefixes, suffixes, vowel sounds, consonant blends, etc.
7. Create a silly sentence using as many of your spelling words as you can. Make as many silly sentences as you need to use up all your words. Underline your spelling words in each sentence.
8. Create a word tower, writing your words from shortest to longest and lining up the middle letters (or middles of the words.)
9. Using the dictionary, write a definition for each of your spelling words.
10. Using a dictionary, write the part of speech for each of your spelling words.

As you can see, these spelling cards of ours practiced much more in the way of language skills than simply the spelling of the words. For numbers 9 and 10, the student has to write the word and then the definition or part of speech after it, so that spelling practice is actually performed. (I have one little fellow who would conveniently "forget" to write the words, too.)

Other ideas for using your children's own misspellings take a bit more time on the part of the parent. There are many sources for creating word searches, crosswords, fill-ins and other puzzles using your own word lists. There's even a website (it costs, though) that allows the teacher to type in a list for each week, and then the program creates various computer games that practice the words as the child plays. You can hold family spelling bees, too, if you have the time and inclination. My daughter used to love spelling her words using magnetic letters on the side of the refrigerator when she was younger. (Alright, I don't suppose that takes much parental time, unless it's to make sure the letters are all put away properly and the fridge is clean enough for them to stick.)

When using your child's own words, regardless of how you practice them, you'll need to test for mastery in some way. I've used the old stand-by spelling test on Friday. I've used crossword puzzles (especially if one of the week's practice cards was the dictionary definitions one. I've used the silly sentence practice as a test, assuming that the child could spell the words correctly while using them if she had learned them during the week. I've even simply pulled a practice card and used whatever it was (unless it was #10) in some way to test for correct spelling. Any words that were missed at the end of the week went back on the list (at the bottom, so as not to bore the children by making them study the same words for two weeks) for studying another time.

Word Families

Using word families to teach spelling has the added benefit of typically improving reading abilities as well. The reader gains confidence and mastery of "big" words through having used them in spelling. You simply start with a two letter word – AT for example. Then you add all the initial consonants possible – BAT, CAT, FAT, HAT, MAT, PAT, RAT, SAT, TAT,

VAT. Next, you add endings – S, ED, ER, ING, etc. wherever possible to make new words within your family. So, your next set of words might include BATTER, CATS, FATTED, and MATTING. Once those are learned, introduce "extra" letters that make even more new words – BRAT, THAT, FLAT. Work up to longer words that contain your core family – BATTLE, PRATTLING, FLATTEN, etc. When you've spent several weeks exploring one word family, move on to another one and repeat the process. You need not spend an entire week on one list of words, either. The typical student picks up the core family words and their spelling pattern quite quickly, making learning endings and extra letters and longer words quite easy, one the "root" family is established.

Some of the "progressive" spellers used in the 19th and early 20th century public schools used this method to teach spelling with great success. There's no reason why a first grader must be limited to three or four letter words, just because that's her mastered reading ability. If she can use a word, there's nothing stopping her from learning to spell the word, too. And once she has learned to read it through spelling practice, she'll add it to her list of known words, quickly and easily improving her reading abilities with unknown words within the same word family. Nice bonus to good spelling, eh?

One of the drawbacks many parents find when trying to teach spelling using word families is that there are few resources for doing so. There are a few books that present the eighty or so root families in some sort of orderly fashion, but many are either expensive, or are geared toward professional educators. There are a few websites, but they aren't always reliable or complete. To that end, in the Appendix, you'll find a starter list of word families. I say starter list because time and space do not allow me to delve fully into each family, but it should be enough to get you started, should you choose this method to teach your children spelling.

Never, regardless of the method you choose for teaching spelling, allow a spelling error to go unchecked and uncorrected. The purpose of teaching spelling is so that children learn to spell correctly. Allowing misspelled words to remain misspelled runs risks of the student mis-learning the word with the incorrect spelling. Then, the tougher job of relearning the word correctly must take place at some later time. All spelling errors in dictations, both initial and final, all spelling errors in the week's copywork or practice exercises, should be corrected immediately by the student for correct spellings to be cemented in the student's mind. I don't recommend really starting spelling instruction with children before 8 years of age or so. Their language abilities should be focused on learning to read, write and enjoyably experience language – phonics, handwriting, composition and creative writing, literature (read alouds,) and memorization – and not worrying them with the nitty-gritty stuff like proper spelling. They'll not be doing much assigned independent writing at this age, anyway, so spelling instruction is a bit unnecessary in my book.

Grammar

To many a former classroom dweller, grammar is almost a dirty word, a nasty subject that conjures up nightmares of long, dull hours spent on mindless exercises of endless sentence diagramming and teachers' red pens. It can be none of the above, though for older children, sentence diagramming can be a good language-based critical thinking exercise. Grammar need not be a series of dry worksheets or meaningless exercises as interesting as peeling paint.

All that is needed to create an effective grammar program is good literature, perhaps a grammar handbook (if it's not your strongest point) and pen and paper. And yes, I actually *do* know of parents out there teaching their children using those seemingly meager materials. And they're doing so in a much more meaningful and interesting way than paint-peeling workbooks and dry, dull texts.

A great deal of punctuation, the parts of speech, parts of a sentence (clauses, phrases, objects, etc.) types of sentences, word usage, subject-verb agreement, verb tenses, plural forms and most of the other mechanics of writing that we lump together under the term GRAMMAR can be taught through dictation exercises. As you use dictation to teach spelling through repeated practice, you can also be using the same passage to teach a grammar concept. Here's how we do it:

Monday – read the passage until the child can read it by himself. Then, do an initial dictation. Spelling errors are pointed out and corrected. Then, the initial dictation is put into the language notebook until Tuesday.

Tuesday – the dictation passage is brought out, read, and the grammar, mechanics and usage of the passage are studied for both the concepts that we know, and the one new concept I want to teach that week. That concept is then pointed out, usually by underlining or circling in colored ink or pencil. A lesson is given on that concept and the child is then allowed to continue with his copywork practice of the passage.

Wednesday – the passage is again brought out, read, and any expanding upon the concept is then done. For example, a passage with quite a few conjunctions might lead to the creation of a more complete list of them in addition to the ones used. Or a passage that includes a title, proper name with initials or other abbreviations can naturally be used to introduce one or more of those concepts. The lists or rules learned are written down and added to the grammar section of our notebooks, and then the child continues with his copywork of the passage.

Thursday – the passage is brought out, read and then the student gets to be the teacher. He has to explain the grammar concept for the week to me. The passage's markings – circlings, underlinings, etc. are still there to serve as visual clues, but the rules and lists are kept hidden away in the notebook until after my "lesson" is over. Then, they are brought out and reviewed. After, the child goes on with his daily copywork.

Friday – the final dictation of the passage is taken. Afterward, a different passage is presented that exemplifies that week's grammar. The child is asked to point out, either orally or by marking the passage, the concept studied all week. If a similar passage can't be found, I'll simply ask the child to write a passage that uses that week's grammar. The passage is reviewed and any necessary corrections made. If significant corrections are necessary, that concept is marked for further teaching in the future. If not, then review can occur naturally anytime that concept is found in future passages.

Choosing passages for their grammar possibilities is actually easier than choosing them for their spelling usage. You can, however, focus on the spelling possibilities of a passage and take whatever grammar comes your way. Either way, you only need one passage per week. As my children copy their passages throughout the week, I encourage them to use colored ink or pencils to mark the grammar concept, much as we've done on Tuesday. That way, they are reinforcing the learning and cementing those concepts without a chance of making a mistake or mis - learning anything. Of course, the same rules for dictation that were laid out in the spelling section above apply to the dictation lessons used for teaching grammar.

Oral and Written Exercises

The purpose of learning grammar is, of course, to have the ability to use language properly when speaking and writing. So, using oral and written exercises in addition to dictation to teach grammar makes perfect sense. Here are some ideas fro creative oral or written lessons:

- Create lists of nouns, verbs and other parts of speech. Make them topical, or alphabetical.
- Call out a word and ask for a synonym or antonym (or homonym if writing.)
- Call out a verb and ask for a past or future or other tense.
- Have them write five sentences. Then, ask them to replace all the nouns, or adjectives, or objects, or *whatever* with new ones.
- Brainstorm lists of 12 prepositional phrases, nouns, and verbs. Roll two dice and use the number rolled to determine the phrase, noun and verb you'll use to construct nonsensical sentences.
- Take all the nouns in a story and change them from singular to plural, and vice versa. Or change them all into pronouns.
- Make a rule that all personal pronouns are banished for a day, or during dinner, or for the trip to grandma's house. Every time a personal pronoun would be used, the full name or first name of the individual being referred to must be used instead. Everyone must play along, of course.
- Assign each punctuation mark its own sound effect. Take turns reading a passage or story. Every time a punctuation mark occurs, the sound effect is used to denote it to the listeners.
- Take a passage from literature. Type it up, removing all the verbs, or adjectives, or prepositions. Replace them with blanks.

Have the children come up with new ones to create a much funnier passage than the original.

Another fun activity my children enjoy using are the Mad Libs books. These books ask for various parts of speech in a list on one page. Then, those numbered words are placed into a story on the back side of the list. The result is usually a hilariously funny story, with giggles and groans abounding. I can sometimes find them for a dollar or two, while my local bookstore carries "omnibus" versions with several books in one. Giggles and grammar? You bet!

If using oral lessons and word games to teach grammar leaves you concerned about documentation or record-keeping, keep "score" as you play by writing things down as you go. You can have the children copy the lists or sentences you've created, either as you go or afterward. Or you can simply denote "language games" or "oral lessons" and the concepts you covered while playing. If it makes it easier for you, give each game a name, and then provide your evaluator with a list of the games, denoting them in your records by their names.

As with spelling, I try to keep the written lessons in grammar to a minimum for the youngest students. Their handwriting and reading skills simply aren't up to the task of a great deal of written exercises. Therefore, language games and oral lessons are much more appropriate. You can point out ending punctuations, initial capitals, complete sentences, types of sentences and whatnot simply while reading their favorite stories. Making lists of words, creating silly sentences, devising original tongue twisters, sharing silly poems and word plays are all fun and easy ways to play with language and to use language in ways that do not require tiring little hands or taxing young minds.

Sentence Diagramming

Sentence diagramming can be a useful tool for analyzing language and for reviewing grammar concepts, but I believe that it should be used with older students, say 12 to 14 year olds and up only, and that the student should be given the diagrams **_with_** the sentences. Explain what goes where and why and then see if they can pick apart the sentences and properly complete the diagrams. Whenever you start diagramming, start slow and start simply, with sentences you know your child can analyze. Then, move on into more difficult grammatical territory, testing her grammar muscles. If you hit a roadblock, go back and review the part of speech causing the problem. By 12 or 14, though, I would expect most students who have had regular and steady grammar lessons to know most, if not all, of the parts of speech and how they are used, and therefore few roadblocks should be met.

I prefer to use sentence diagramming as a review or even as a "test" of the grammar we've learned, rather than as an exercise in *teaching* or *practicing* that grammar. There's a wonderful scene in Laura Ingalls Wilder's *Little Town on the Prairie* where she is asked to diagram a complex sentence as part of her teacher's certification examination. It's to prove she knows proper grammar, not to see if she knows how to diagram. I believe that's what diagramming is really for and how it should be used. It's too easy to turn diagramming from an exercise in grammar into an exercise in drudgery just because that's all we've ever experienced with diagramming before.

Literature and Poetry

Literature and poetry are possibly the easiest language arts components to teach on the cheap. All you need is a library, either public or at home, that's well stocked with age-appropriate quality literature, and a notebook. The process is simple.

1. Create a booklist. There are many, many good sources for creating booklists. There are recommended reading lists, required reading lists, "good book" reading lists – for nearly any age and reading ability. Your local library may have some, your local school district should have some, curriculum catalogs are full of titles, and the Internet is full of booklists of every type and description. Consider your child's age, reading level and interests when creating your lists every term, along with the intended purpose behind your literature program. (More on this in a bit.)
2. Give your child the list and a log sheet for recording the titles she reads. (If your child isn't reading independently yet, you may want to keep this list and log yourself.)

3. Give the student a binder with lined paper and at least 4 dividers to divide the notebook into 5 sections.
4. In section 1, place the book list and reading log.
5. In section 2, place a number of sheets of paper. Each day, you or the child will read one chapter. After reading, the child will either dictate a narration to you, or will write a short narration, summarizing the chapter, characters, etc. (Use your narration starters here, if you like, or simply ask for a short summary.) Each narration/summary, should be dated and labeled with the chapter's name or number, on a page with the title at the top. When one title is finished, start a new page for the next title.
6. Section 3 is for vocabulary. Any word encountered during reading that the child doesn't know, or has to figure out the meaning of through context clues, gets written down on a piece of paper with the book's title at the top. The definition is written beside it. Again, the vocabulary pages for each title should be kept separate from other titles.
7. Section 4 is for book reports. Once a book is completed, some sort of report should be created. There are many, many kinds of books reports to choose from. A short list of possibilities is in the Appendix. If a non-written, non-paper form of report is done, some sort of note, photograph, etc. of the presentation should be made and included to show that a report was created.
8. Section 5 (optional) is for poetry study. The first page should be a list of poets or poems for the student to choose from, much like your book list. We study a poet in between each literature title, to give ourselves a little break. The student reads poetry instead of her daily chapter for a couple of days. (More on this later, too.)
9. Explain to your student how to use the notebook.
10. Allow the student to choose her first title and begin her daily reading and recording in her notebook.

You've just set your literature program in motion!

    I begin these literature notebooks in full with my children about age 9. Prior to that, I supply them with a booklist, simply let them read and narrate to me, or read and complete some sort of simple book report. Written narrations are best started after a child is comfortable with handwriting, and has some experience, however small, with short compositions. Even summary of a sentence or two might seem daunting to a 7 or 8 year old. Also, many children may not have the skills to find the context clues for unknown words, or the reading ability to tackle chapter books. You can start earlier, of course, depending on your child's abilities. You might be able to take oral dictations, and choose vocabulary words for your child, and select their poets and poems for study. To me, this was just added work for me. I prefer to wait until the children can make the choices, find their own definitions (they remember them better that way, anyway) and do much of the work independently.

Vocabulary

After your child has accumulated 10 vocabulary words, you should require her to use them in some sort of vocabulary exercises. (I adapted a few of the spelling exercises for our vocabulary practice.) After a week or so of practice, test his vocabulary knowledge by asking him to use each word correctly in a sentence. Then, repeat when another ten words have built up on the list. Every 30 words, devise a review week, and then choose 10 words at random to assure retention of the new vocabulary. Depending on your child's existing vocabulary and reading level, it may take several weeks to acquire each set of ten words, so regular review is helpful.

If the list fills too quickly, within the first few days, the title is probably too difficult for your reader. It may be best to set it aside for a later try, after some reading and vocabulary advancements have been made. We use the five finger rule. If the child encounters 5 unknown or "have to figure it out" words within the first 5 pages, the title is set aside and a different one is chosen. For this reason, I always have my children choose at least two titles from their booklist at a time, in case one turns out to be too "heady" in its choice of vocabulary. (Classic literature, even classic children's literature, is often sprinkled with "five dollar" words, sometimes very liberally sprinkled, and even a fairly good reader can sometimes encounter a classic title that causes difficulties.)

Likewise, if the list fills much too slowly, say an entire title goes by with no "new" words, then you may want to consider some more challenging titles for your list, or you may want to simply assign some vocabulary words from each title. My daughter has a very high reading level, and often claims not to find any new words because she has reached the point where she can figure out unknown words fairly quickly and easily. She doesn't always think to write these words down, because in her mind, in a few seconds after encountering them, she has deciphered what they mean. So, for her, I find a few words per title and add them to her vocabulary list, or in many cases she wouldn't have a vocabulary list from which to work!

Poetry Study

As I mentioned in step 8 of the Literature notebook, we have a section devoted to poets and their poetry. We take two or three days off from reading in between each title, and spend it reading poetry and learning about the poet(s) behind it. I've found the *Poetry for Young Children* series of titles invaluable for our poetry studies, as they typically include a short biography of the poet before the actual poetry selections begin, and I can be assured that the poetry selected is appropriate for my children. Other good sources are *The Harp and the Laurel Wreath*, *The Random House Book of Poetry for Children*, *Favorite Poems of Childhood* and *Favorite Poems Old and New*. Any good public library should have at least some of these, or you can make an investment in one or more of them. (They will be useful for years and years, even after the children are grown, as one never really outgrows good poetry.) Our poet lists for each age group are included in the Appendix, but you can create your own to suit your tastes and needs.

I allow my children to choose a poet from their list, and to spend a day or two reading poems by their selected poet. Then, they complete a simply biography report on their poet and choose one poem to "study." I have them copy their poem (or at least two stanzas) out on lined paper. We mark the rhyme scheme, if there is one, at the end of each line with standard lettering (abba, for example.) We circle the sounds involved in any assonance or alliteration, find similes and imagery, look for regular meter, etc. (We don't do it all every time. I choose a different element of poetry to work on for each study.) I also point out, if applicable, the specific type of poem they've chosen – sonnet, epic, free verse, etc. to familiarize them with the various forms of poetry out there. Whenever possible, if there is a significant event or person tied to the poem or poet, we'll briefly discuss that, as well. We write all this down in the notebook. As a last step in our study, I give the child the option of writing their own poem in the style of the chosen study piece. Sometimes they do, sometimes they don't. It's never a requirement, though.

We don't pick every poem apart for meaning or symbolism, though. I don't want them to lose the joy of poetry, just to learn enough of the "guts" of poetry to possibly write their own poems, and to understand poetry a little better when faced with a more in-depth study or discussion later.

In this way, we can study and enjoy 6 or more poets and their poetry each year, depending on the length of the books my children choose. My daughter discovered Edgar Allen Poe in her fifth grade year and went around quoting *The Raven* for at least two weeks and now has a passion for Robert Frost and his works, while my son delighted in *Father William* and other Lewis Carroll pieces even longer than his sister croaked "Nevermore."

You need not be a poetry expert to impart a love and knowledge of poetry in your children. <u>Rhyme scheme</u> is simply the pattern of rhyming words at the end of each line. The first line is "a" and every other line in the poem that rhymes with it is also marked "a." The next rhyme is marked "b" and all of its rhyming lines are also "b"s. The next is "c" and so forth on through the poem. (Certain poems, like sonnets, are determined by their rhyme schemes.) <u>Assonance</u> is the use of vowel sounds within a line of poetry to create hidden or inner rhyme. <u>Alliteration</u> is the repetition of the same initial or beginning sound or sounds within and across lines of poetry. <u>Consonance</u> is the repetition of the same sound, wherever it might occur in the words. (Alliteration is in fact a special form of consonance.) <u>Meter</u> is the basic rhythmic structure of a line or series of lines. (Look for the stressed and unstressed syllables. Reading the poem out loud helps with this.) We denote stressed syllables with a little "+" overtop. Regular meter will have a set pattern, either the same number of stressed and unstressed syllables, or the same pattern to the stressed and unstressed syllables. Irregular meter will not have these patterns. You can educate yourself and your children about things like iambic pentameter, and other kinds of special poetic meters, or you can simply find the meter (or lack thereof.) That goes for other aspects of poetry that you may not be well-versed in. It really depends on how in-depth and complex you want your poetry studies to be. I prefer simple and enjoyable. Either way, you'll still be learning a great deal about poets and their works, and exposing your children to a wonderful portion of literature they might not otherwise experience.

Purpose of Your Literature Program

The purpose of your literature program will greatly influence your choice of titles for your children's booklists. If all you want is to expose your children to good quality literature, your job of selecting titles should be fairly easy. You need look no further than the Newberry Medal and Honor Medal winners, or a similar awards list. Likewise, if you wish to introduce them to the "classics" of children's literature, lists of classic titles are very easy to come. If your aim is top create a varied literature program, with titles from several different genres, it may take a bit more work and effort on your part to research age and ability appropriate titles to suit your needs. You can also use your literature program to enhance your history or science programs, too. Naturally, finding enough titles to do so might require greater effort, too. You may just need to use your literature program as I do – to ensure that your children read something other than science fiction, or mysteries, or spy novels, or whatever it is your children are "stuck" on this year!

Memorization

I realize that not all homeschoolers see a need for memorization. I also realize that this debate can become heated and nasty in some homeschooling circles. I, personally, see a merit to *some* memorization taking place. By *some* I mean we memorize poetry, Scripture verses and passages, quotations from famous people and pieces of literature, folk sayings and proverbs, and maxims. I don't require a great deal of memorizing of *facts* – dates, names, figures, etc. Enough repetition and exposure to important people, events and ideas typically secures the facts in my children's minds without having to require them to memorize much of anything. Since our memorization takes a more literary form, therefore, I've added it here to the language arts chapter instead of elsewhere.

I assign one memorization passage, on average, per month. If possible, I make the selection timely – either seasonal or topical – to what we are studying or living at the time. I try to stick to the rule of thumb of two lines per year of age, although sometimes the selection will be just a tad longer or shorter. If a child wants a greater challenge (and sometimes they do) then I'll be more than happy to oblige them!

We begin by reading the selection, several times. Then, the child is required to read it several times a day for the first week. The next three weeks are given over to both daily reading and writing (if the selection is very long, we'll break it up into daily "bites" to make it easier to copy out.) I often allow memorization selections to be used as copywork for the day, killing two birds with one stone. The final week is devoted to preparations for the final recitation and written presentation. The child is asked to recite their selection from memory, and then to write it from memory. The written memorization goes into the section of the notebook devoted to memory work. (We don't save "practice" pages unless they serve as daily copywork, in which case they are filed in the copywork portion of the notebook.) If the selection is in a book that is used for more than just memorization, or is used by more than one member of our homeschool, I will type it out or the child will copy it out. I also type up any particularly long passages, so they can be read and copied more easily. These are temporarily stored in the notebook's memory section until the final page is completed.

You may feel that four weeks is too long for a single memorization assignment. The purpose of memorizing things, in my opinion, is to store them away for future enjoyment or practical use. Shorter assignment times tend to pressure my children, leading to incomplete, incorrect, or quickly forgotten memorizations. This defeats my purpose entirely. Therefore, I give them a longer period of time to digest and internalize the selections assigned to them, so that they can truly take them to heart.

Miscellaneous Skills

There are bits of language learning that don't really seem to fit in any one category, or cross categories, but should not go unaddressed. Things like library skills, research skills, speaking skills, note taking and letter writing can be easily added to your language arts program, either as they are needed, or just here and there, with just a little effort and planning.

Library Skills

Take opportunity of your next trip to the local library to introduce the Dewey decimal system for non-fiction books; the library's card catalog or computerized catalog system; how to place a book on reserve; how to request an InterLibrary loan; where in the library you might find the music or video selections, books on tape, or periodicals; or any other library-related skill or knowledge that comes to mind to need. Some of this may come up naturally, as you or your children want a specific title, or are studying a certain subject. (This is what I like to call organic learning – they learn because they need to know and they need to know *now*.)

Something that I've done with my own children is to devise library "scavenger hunts." For the Dewey decimal system, for example, I created several sheets asking them to find titles within a certain topic, or titles within a certain "hundred" within the system. I also gave them the call numbers and asked them to find specific titles or topics. (All without using the library's computerized catalog, of course.) In this way they quickly became familiarized with the non-fiction section of the children's library, and my daughter was even able to carry that knowledge into the general non-fiction shelves when a title she needed for a research project turned out to be a "grown up" book. Other scavenger hunts have included asking them to find me one title from each of the library's specialized collections. (This varies from library to library, but I figure if they can navigate our public library's special collections, if they can't find something on another library's general shelves, they'll know to look or ask for the location of special collections. Our library's special collections include new titles, mysteries, large print editions, mass paperbacks, audiobooks, books by authors from our state, and oversized editions. They also have seasonal collections that are changed throughout the year, so that in December for example, you'll find *A Christmas Carol* not in its usual place, but on the shelf with other holiday reading, while in July "patriotic reading" may take center stage. For this reason, I had the children do several "collections" hunts.) Our library has a special coding system that they use for shelving music selections, too, so I made up a hunt sheet that had the children using the color-codes to find certain CD's, composers, types of music and various artists. Regardless of the quality of your local library, knowing how to use it will aid your children in using other, larger libraries in the future. Library skills are too important, therefore, not to teach.

Research Skills

Research skills, for the most part, are best taught as they are needed. Dictionary skills can be learned as a child learns to spell or define new words. Assigning reports on animals, people, states or countries, and significant historical events afford many opportunities to teach your children how to locate the necessary information. The final written report will require organizing and recording that information, as well as producing a well-thought out presentation of the things they've learned. When they are old enough, proper citing of the sources of their information should be required, too.

I know some parents of non-college-bound students feel that teaching proper citation or the creating of a bibliography is not necessary. I disagree, unless the child has some special need that prevents them from ever furthering their education.

1.) You can't tell if your child will *never* attend some form of higher education at *any* point in their lifetime just because they have no interest in attending now. They may find a need or desire to attend as an adult student later, and even though styles or preferred methods may have changed, at least they've had experience with the concept of creating a bibliography for their writings.

2.) They will need to know how to *read* bibliographies if they ever wish to research a topic on their own, as they are often included as "further reading" in books and articles, as well as serving as the basis for the content included in those books and articles.

3.) Writing a bibliography is an exercise in critical thinking, if nothing else.

Whether your research is conducted the old-fashioned way, with books and papers, or is completely digitized, you'll want to help your student so that she knows how to find the most relevant information, and find it quickly. I find the use of "guided" research is best for this. Our guided research begins with simple, fill-in forms. Complete the form and the research is done, as well as the report. Over time, the forms become more and more complex, and emptier, requiring much more information and more writing by the student. Eventually, we've progressed from filling in forms to simply writing out the information on paper to create a written report. It's taken several years for my daughter to reach this point, but she can now construct a well-planned, well-presented report with ease and confidence.

Speaking Skills

Oral language lessons, reading aloud, recitations, oral narrations and oral presentations of book and research reports will go a long way to improving and advancing your students' speaking skills. To add another dimension, the next time he disagrees with a house rule or parental decision, allow him to create a speech or debate, in an attempt to persuade you to see his side of the matter. Help him craft a persuasive and cohesive speech, and allow him to present it one night after dinner, or one Sunday afternoon. You could arrange an evening or afternoon of recitations, dramatic readings and other oral presentations for neighbors, relatives or house guests. Perhaps your religious organization has opportunities for public reading or speaking that your children could become involved in. (We use lectors every service to read the day's Scripture passages.)

Never allow poor grammar or word usage in your children's speech, please. Correcting these "small" errors when they occur will create proper speech (and writing, too) in a short time. My children now point out the poor grammar of radio presenters, television characters and even a prominent leader during one of his speeches – I'd say my speaking skills lessons are paying off.

Note Taking

There are two types of note taking – taking notes from written sources and taking notes from speakers – which children should know how to do. At the ages we're covering in this book, the simplest, basic form of note taking is all that should be required, except for our oldest children.

Notes taken from written sources vary greatly depending on the information one desires to preserve. You might teach highlighting of a text, finding the most relevant idea in each paragraph and underlining, copying or using a highlighting pen to pull it out and set it off. You may want to teach summarizing, where a short sentence or two sums up each paragraph. You might teach fact-detail finding – sorting through each sentence to see if it presents a fact, or a supporting detail of that fact. The facts are written on separate cards (or in separate lists) and then their supporting details written beneath them or on the opposite side of the card. I've taught all of the above, using activities similar to our guided research, asking the child to find the relevant information and record it in the appropriate manner. In my opinion, the hardest part of researching and note taking is discerning just what the relevant information of any one piece actually *is*. Guiding my children through their research helps them to discover relevancy, and consequently helps them develop this skill.

Notes from speakers are harder to take, unless the speaker uses some sort of printed, written or projected outline. Think of the last sermon or homily, the last televised speech, the last presentation you attended. How much could you remember? How much could you jot down? Our children find it even harder, as they can't write that fast to begin with, often have a hard time focusing their attentions, and often can't figure out what the most important points happen to be. I've found that pretend scenarios help. I'll give a few sentence "presentation" and then ask them to orally tell me what the most important thing I said was. We slowly work up to longer "speeches" – still only asking for oral narrations, as it were. Then, we go back to the beginning, with shorter proclamations, but this time the student is asked to write down their "important point." As the speeches become longer, they realize that they will miss things if they don't write as I'm speaking, so they start jotting their own notes – often just a word or two to jog their memories when I've finished. We're not past 5 or 6 sentences yet, but we're working our way slowly. And as we go, my daughter is devising her own form of note taking that seems to work for her.

Ultimately, note taking skills become personal – we all have our own little ways that work best for us. Whether or not those ways are something we've been taught or something that we, like my daughter, have discovered along the way, doesn't really seem to matter in the end. The purpose of teaching note taking is so that your child has the ability to record information for future reference, either personal as in the case of a sermon, or academic or professional as in the case of a research paper or written report. However that purpose is accomplished isn't as important as that it is accomplished.

Letter Writing

Letter writing is a skill which the computer age has actually made more important, in my opinion. Emails may have replaced good old fashioned stamp and envelope letters, but they need not replace properly formed messages. Business correspondence is still business correspondence, while personal messages are still personal messages. And in this day and age of fewer letters in the mail box, a personal note is a welcome gift.

We begin with simple "thank you" notes for birthday and holiday gifts, visits from friends, and other thoughtful gestures. Then, we progress to monthly letters to distant friends and relatives. (Some live as "far away" as a few miles up the road!) Around 9 or 10, we learn to craft letters of inquiry, most often to authors of our favorite books, asking about our favorite titles or any new, upcoming projects they may have in mind. Older children can learn to compose letters to the editor around issues that concern them; letters of complaint for faulty or shoddy products or service; and letters of support or concern to politicians and other leaders. By combining opportunities that Real Life presents you, and a little planning, you'll find chances for composing both personal and professional letters abound.

Keyboarding

As a writer, my keyboard is both my best friend and my worst enemy. I spend far too many hours with it, leading to a love-hate relationship. Knowing how to use it, though, is an invaluable skill in today's world. Teaching my children how to use it is essential to their future.

There are many free resources for teaching keyboarding on the Internet. There are games, complete courses, bells-and-whistle programs, and bare-bones instruction. Everyone from the youngest student to the oldest beginner can find something to suit their needs and tastes. Some public libraries have "how to" programs on their public use computers, and instruction books on their shelves. Inexpensive software is available for purchase from many sources. My only advice is to start young and practice often. Speed and accuracy are the goals, and they are only reached through diligent, patient practice. My children have progressed through several programs, all free, but they still have a long way to go. Be sure that your program is:

- Age appropriate – not too difficult nor too "babyish"
- Moves at an appropriate pace – not too fast nor too slow
- Provides some way of reviewing skills already learned – either through specific reviews or through constant review as the program progresses
- Provides some way of ensuring mastery by not moving on until the skill can be performed at a certain speed or level of accuracy or both

If you find that you need more than one program to turn your children into confident, competent typists, don't worry. The review and practice they receive will be invaluable.

Language Notebooks

Our language arts notebooks have sections for each of the portions of language arts – composition, copywork, spelling/dictation, grammar, creative writing, memorization, and miscellaneous skills. Note that reading is not included here. I don't use notebooks for phonics instruction, so it isn't necessary, and as you've seen, our literature is kept separate. (If you create or use worksheets or games for phonics, then you may want to add a section for it.) Once your student is 9 or 10, use the grammar section for writing down grammar rules, word lists, and punctuation guides, as they are learned. (I mentioned doing so in our notebooks in the grammar section.) As they learn and study, they will create their own grammar or writer's handbook to which they refer whenever a question or uncertainty arises. I don't require dictation practices to be filed in the notebooks, only the initial and final papers. In our memorization section, you'll find the selections written from memory on some sort of special papers. My daughter likes to decorate her final memorization pages, while my son prefers pre-printed papers I make on the computer for him. Not only does this produce a nice portfolio of the year's language learning, but it also can serve, as in the case of the grammar guidebook, for future reference.

If you choose to use your student's own misspellings as your spelling program, be careful what else you do with those creative writing exercises. Having them in the notebook makes them easy reference at the end of the week, but picking them apart for every offense is a sure-fire way to stifle creativity. I stopped using my children's own misspelled words for spelling because I went too far by using them for grammar lessons, too. I went from receiving wonderfully creative, complex responses to journal prompts and creative writing exercises to seeing a few sentences or a few short paragraphs, because they were afraid of making too many mistakes. Journals and creative writings should only be used for finding misspelled words – not for every missed period, or misplaced comma, or dangling participle. I never use them for grammar lessons anymore, unless it's a Friday passage to mark or orally discuss, and then I've retyped or rewritten it with no errors. Their creative work is too precious, too personal, to trample on with corrections and grammar lessons. Now, I'm back to pages and pages of stories and poems and essays that really shed light on my children's creative abilities, and their hearts and minds, too.

Conclusion

Language arts on the cheap are perhaps the most teacher-time-intensive of all the subjects in your school day. The most time spent, for me anyway, is in finding selections for dictation and memorization exercises. Don't let this deter you from settling for the Curriculum Craziness of expensive purchased packages. Begin to read children's literature with one eye on your scope and sequence and the other open for possibilities for lesson material. Include fun and interesting games and activities to take the place of dull worksheets and drill exercises. Don't be afraid to try dictation and narration. They'll seem awkward at first, but they'll easily become an integral part of your week. Your children's literature notebooks will become almost automatic – they won't dream of reading their literature selections without their notebooks by their sides. Scavenger hunts and word games can make learning enjoyable and sharable. Remember, a good foundation in language skills is vital to the success of your children, and in most cases, of your homeschool. It's well worth stepping out of your comfort zone to try some new and different ideas. It's also well worth every moment spent making it work!

∞ ∞ ∞

Maths

No More Math Wimps Allowed!

Our scene opens with the author rising from her seat, raising her right hand skyward, and tentatively announcing, "Hello, my name is Suz, and I'm a Math Wimp."

There, I've said it, and declared it publicly, too. We're not always easy to find, we Math Wimps. We've devised many clever and cunning ways to hide our wimpiness. We usually attach ourselves to Wimpiness Enablers, too, in the loved ones with whom we share our lives and gladly, sometimes unknowingly, cover for us. We're the ones whose husbands balance the checkbooks or who let wives keep the family budget and pay the bills. We use calculators an computer spreadsheets to do the heavy lifting for us. Yet our Math Wimpiness eventually catches up to us at some point, especially when we begin to homeschool.

Homeschooling Math Wimps are the ones who wouldn't dare even dream of teaching our children math without a full-blown curriculum. We plunk down large sums of money for the programs with DVD lessons and/or computer tutors to further release us from the responsibilities of actually teaching math. You'll find us sympathizing with the trials and tears of our children, because we remember al too well the torments we suffered at the hands of our math teachers and textbooks. We marvel at all those Math Machos who can strike out on their own, abandoning their teachers' manuals and scripted lesson plans. The kind of confidence and bravery they display as they sally forth armed only with a scope and sequence and not spiral reviews is beyond our capability to comprehend. We are Math Wimps – and we need help!

Since Math Wimps Anonymous has yet to catch on, many of us sorely afflicted individuals feel we must bravely soldier on, textbook in one hand and DVD tutor in the other, dependent on others to do the teaching for us, addicted to our curriculum. We stick with programs that aren't quite a good fit for us or our children because we lack the confidence to do anything different. Or, worse yet, we switch from program to program, desperately seeking just the *right one* while our children gradually lose patience with us, and confidence in their own mathematical abilities. It doesn't take long before a new generation of Math Wimps is born, as our children learn not math, but that math is something to be feared or suffered through.

It needn't be that way, though. There is hope to be had and help to be found on the steps of the living math path! Care to join me? Brave enough to admit that you, too are a Math Wimp? Would you vow with me to break the cycle of textbook addiction? Stand up and declare, "No more Math Wimps allowed!"

Like using living books – real words, "real" books – to teach language arts, living math is much more natural, fun and effective. Living math replaces textbooks with real books – some literary with characters, plots and everything, some more math oriented. It replaces worksheets with math journals and a few daily review problems. It substitutes drill with puzzles and games, drudgery with exploration and active learning, tests and quizzes with real life experiences. In short, all those things Math Wimps see Math Machos adding to their days, or have in fact added to their own days in an effort to math their textbook-workbook program more enjoyable, understandable or simply more palatable for their children, it's a good bet you'll find it among the wealth of resources available on the Living Math Path!

The Facts About Math

There are some of you, my fellow Math Wimps, out there right now shaking in your shoes. *Math without worksheets? She's lost her mind! No teacher's manual, no textbooks? Preposterous! No flashcards, tests, spiral reviews? You've got to be JOKING!* I know. I was right there, quivering alongside you, once upon a time. Then, I sat down to compare math programs, yet again, in an effort to find something my Math Wimpy daughter might actually learn from without tears, fears and years of frustration. I was struck by they *all* teach the same things, in pretty much the same order. They all have their own little twists and tweaks, of course, but I had discovered something Math Machos already know –math is math is math. Now, I didn't pay much attention to when those different programs taught something, just what it was that they were teaching. I quickly realized that there are less than 2 dozen mathematical topics that should be taught and hopefully mastered before a child enters high school's upper level math. *Less than 2 dozen?* That's it. Even if you take the basic geometry and basic algebra families and consider each of their concepts as separate entities, you'll be hard pressed to come up with more than 30 topics to teach your children before higher maths come calling.

Most of us begin teaching math somewhere around age 4 to 6. If you stop and consider that our children don't have to have their "lower" math concepts mastered until they are somewhere between 14 and 16, we have 10 years to put all this math stuff into their little heads. TEN YEARS! And less than 30 concepts, too! Makes it a little less intimidating now, doesn't it?

Here are the concepts considered essential before a child reaches higher maths:

1. Counting to 100 (after that, it's just repeats of the same, really)
2. Place value – both positive and negative numbers
3. Time
4. Money
5. Addition
6. Subtraction
7. Multiplication
8. Division
9. Decimals
10. Percents
11. Fractions
12. Statistics – graphs, charts, etc.
13. Probability
14. Coordinate graphing
15. Basic algebra
    a. Patterns, classifications and sets
    b. Order of operations
    c. Commutative, Associative and Distributive Properties
    d. Variables
    e. Formulas and equations
    f. Graphing linear equations
16. Exponents – squares, cubes, roots
17. Scientific Notation
18. Basic Geometry
    a. 2 and 3 dimensional shapes
    b. Units of measure – standard and metric
    c. Perimeter
    d. Area
    e. Volume
    f. Angles
    g. Pythagorean Theorem
    h. 3 dimensional surface area

Addition, subtraction, multiplication and division should be taught up to four digits – working with numbers in the thousands. After that, it's like counting, repeats of the same. Also, some algebra programs teach linear graphing in the "pre" algebra year, while others begin with it, so you may want to look into your intended programs scope and sequence before worrying your 14 year old with it.

You'll notice that I use the term "MATHS" every now and then, adding a strange looking "S" to the end. This is something I picked up from a British program my children used for a few years. The Brits (and apparently a good bit of the world, actually) don't view math as one giant, all-encompassing subject. They see it as smaller groups, or families, of skills. Geometry is one family, algebra another. Basic operations and concepts like counting, negatives, fractions, decimals and place value are grouped under Numeracy. Statistics, ratios and probability are another family altogether. Measurements, money, time and distance (the last two of which are really forms of measuring) are either placed with Numeracy skills, or are a separate set I've seen labeled "Life Maths." I find it helps when planning our maths learning to see it not as one giant, all-encompassing behemoth, either, but to take it on smaller groups or families of related skills.

Now, when planning our maths learning every year, I choose 6 or so skill families and focus on each for about 6 weeks. Six weeks of concentrated effort and energy goes a long way to reaching mastery of the skill. Couple that with daily review of skills already learned and you've got a powerful one-two punch in your fight to ready your Math Machos for the world!

The Language of Math

As important as the skills are to higher maths success, don't forget to teach the proper language of math along the way. Some will come naturally – you can't teach fractions without discussing factors, denominators or mixed numbers. Others will need more concerted effort. Our children often lose the concept for the symbols – they know how to divide, but they don't know what to do with that *thing* on the page. *This 2 means that there are two of something, while this + means we must put those two somethings together, and this ≠ means that those two somethings can't be the same two somethings.* In order for anyone to understand, master and apply mathematical concepts they must first have mastered the symbols and structures that make up the language of math. Just like English, Hebrew, Russian and Greek have their own signs and symbols and constructions, so too does math. It's a foreign language to our children (and to many of us Math Wimps, too) and it should be treated as such, with regular review and frequent use. That's another reason why daily reviews are so important. Just as a non-native speaker can only gain mastery of his second language through daily practice of his new tongue, so math language learners must have ample opportunity to read, speak, write, and most importantly *think* in mathematics. So, daily math work or review is a must, in whatever form it takes.

Dailies

We focus on the same skill or family of skills for 6 weeks at a time. During those 6 weeks, however, we are also reviewing skills we've previously covered. I do this by giving my children 5 to 10 daily problems. We call them our "Dailies" to distinguish them from our other ongoing work. It may not sound like much - 5 to 10 problems a day – but it really does work to keep "old" skills fresh and sharp. While my son is focusing on learning multiplication, he's also practicing addition and subtraction with borrowing/carrying over/renaming as he goes. Then, he may spend a week of dailies practicing his skills at reading and using a ruler to measure things, or converting metric lengths into standard units. Or he might spend a few days reviewing geometry vocabulary by naming shapes or angles. In this way, we don't lose all that learning that has taken place in previous terms or even in previous years. And at 5 to 10 problems a day, he's finished his math review and gone off to something else in 5 to 10 minutes. Pretty painless way to keep skill levels up, don't you think?

I find coming up with dailies isn't as much of a chore as it used to be. I choose a concept or skill family to focus on for the week. Then, I sit down with 5 sheets of paper and simply create my dailies pages all at once. If I need inspiration, there are worksheet generators all over the Internet, sample pages from math curricula to "borrow" inspiration from, even free programs and lessons online to use as sources for our daily reviews. If all you need are numbers to use for basic operations, look no further than your weekly sale flyers in the mailbox. Take out the decimal points (or not, as the case may be) and you've found a treasure trove of digits to put together. Living math, like living language arts, does take some time to plan and prepare, but it is time well spent. And as you go along, you'll find yourself spending less and less time in preparation, as you develop your system or routine for preparing your dailies and even your weekly lessons.

Literary Math

Just as not all books can be considered "living" books, not all math books are literary in nature. In fact, it's a safe assumption to say that most math books aren't literary in nature at all. But, that hasn't stopped some intrepid authors from bucking the trend and producing some really solid math books disguised as literature. Some of our favorites are Greg Tang, Cindy Neuschwander, and Kjartan Poskitt. Allow me to introduce Dr. Stanley F. Schmidt as well, who has actually written a maths program for middle and upper level students in a literary style. *Yes, Math Wimps, there is hope!* And then there are the not-so-literary, but still useful, titles from authors who have preferred to concentrate more on the numbers and less on the story. These have a place in your living math household, too. You probably won't find yourselves snuggled up on the sofa with one of the latter type of titles, but that doesn't mean they aren't enjoyable. There's a small list of literary math titles in the Appendix, to get you started no matter where you are on your living math path.

We typically reserve one day every other week for literary math reading. If there are exercises or problems or brain ticklers in the title, we always take the time to complete them, too. Literary math is funny in that there seem to be many more titles for the younger set, just starting out on their living math paths, than there are for the older children. Counting books, adding books, books that introduce fractions, shapes, sorting, measurements, and whatnot fill the library shelves. We've found fewer and fewer books as we've neared the middle and end of our paths. The *Sir Cumference* series of geometry books by Cindy Neuschwander are utterly enjoyable, as are *The Number Devil* and Poskitt's *Murderous Maths* books. But it seems that the older my children become truly literary math books are fewer and harder to find. (That's why we only take one day every other week now, unless we stumble upon a really good chapter book, and then we'll read it more often.)

My point is not to grumble about the lack of good literary titles for older children, but to point out the abundance of literary titles for the younger set, where many Math Wimps first become discovered, in those early years of homeschooling. There is a series of emergent readers, written specifically for beginner readers, with a math theme. There are, as I've mentioned, many books that introduce concepts that can be added to your arsenal of living math supplies. Snuggle up, read a book, work the problems given or make up a few of your own and call it math for the day. Much more pleasant than slogging your way through a teachers' manual and then turning your child loose on a workbook page of 30 or so problems, isn't it?

Math Journals

In much the same way as we keep language arts notebooks and literature notebooks, we keep math journals. Our math journals have six divisions: Responses, Dailies, Hands-On Activities, Puzzlers and Thinkers, Dictionary, and Mini-Offices. Our entire math learning, whether from books, games, daily reviews, or working with our many and varied manipulatives, is recorded in the pages of our math journals.

The responses section is just that, a place to record responses. Responses to what, you might ask? Well, to the problems we encounter in our literary math titles, to prompts I create or find (*Take one scoop of Lego blocks. Sort by colors. Create a bar graph to show your results,*) and to anything else that isn't easily placed in one of the other divisions. We even occasionally have math-related copywork, a quote or a saying, worthy of recording in our response section.

Dailies are, as discussed before, our daily review pages. Keeping them all in one place aids in finding them if I need to refer back to what we did six weeks ago, so I know whether a skill has been reviewed in the recent past, or if it needs to pop up again. Also, sending a child to previous daily pages if he "forgets" is often just the thing needed to jog his memory as to what or how he needs to do something.

We have many different math manipulatives to aid us in our math journey. We have Cuisenaire rods, pattern blocks (no, they are not just for 5 year olds,) pentominoes, tangrams, fraction circles, rulers, compasses, protractors, hundred number boards, Wedgits, geoboards, dominoes and a whole collection of rubber bands, toothpicks, paper clips and dried beans for doing just about anything you could think of. We use our hands-on materials most often when introducing a skill, as the concrete examples they give are best understood at the beginning stages of learning. We also use them to practice skills, building mastery as we "play" our way through our lessons. I didn't buy all our manipulatives at once, though, and neither should you, especially if you're trying to truly homeschool on the cheap. I've built our collection up slowly, over the years. I will say that the most useful have been our rods and our pattern blocks, especially since I found wonderful resource books that show me how to use these two groups of items to teach concepts all the way up through middle school! (The titles are listed in the Appendix.) We also do a great deal of real life math, which is explained in some detail later, and those activities are recorded here, too.

Puzzlers and Thinkers are brain teasers I find (sometimes my children find them, too) in books, on websites, in the newspaper, or in puzzle books. Who doesn't enjoy a good head scratcher every now and then? And when you can use them to exercise math skills as well, all the better! Sometimes I write them out, sometimes the children copy them out. Either way, they are placed at the top of the page and the answers are worked out below. We've found toothpick puzzles, number squares, logic puzzles, even puzzles that use calculators to find the answers. Keep your eyes open, or do a concerted search, and you'll find more than you and your children can probably complete in a year.

As we go through our maths learning, we have a special place in our journals reserved for the language of math. In our dictionaries, we begin with 26 sheets of lined paper, one for each letter of the alphabet. As we come across definitions, terms, symbols, etc. in our lessons, we add them to the appropriate page. This creates an instant learning aid, a handy reference tool, for those times when the language gets in the way of the concept.

Lastly, we have a section of our math journal reserved for our mini-offices. Mini-Offices have been around in classrooms for years, but are just now making their way into the homeschooling world. Simply put, a mini-office is a collection of "cheat sheets" – pages that a child can turn to for help with solving a problem or jogging her memory. Our mini-offices are home to our multiplication charts; examples of how to work long division; a fraction comparison chart; the associative, distributive and commutative properties in action; even a small table showing the names and examples of different types of graphs, in case someone forgets just I meant when I said to graph the Lego block sort in a bar graph. In short, it's a place to put all those little "helps" a student may need, things she may forget or need close to hand. Instead of the file folder most commonly used by classroom dwellers, I've printed our components out and pasted them to cardstock pages, for easier storage in the notebooks. As the years go on, the mini-offices have changed, leaving numbers lines to aid in counting, and the parts of a fraction, and other lower level math concepts far behind. Your mini-office will be determined by your student's abilities and your current lesson focus. It's a bit organic, in a way, growing and changing as your child develops and grows.

I suppose I should mention one little tip that I've learned over the years – graph paper isn't just for graphs anymore! All of our dailies are done on graph paper – 4 lines to an inch. The squares make the perfect place to place the digits of the numbers in the problems, allowing children to keep place values in their proper places. Even word problems can be written on graph paper, giving the student the boxes or squares for writing his own problems. No more sloppy math papers to correct! And no more confusion over whether that 2 is in the thousands or in the hundreds place, so no more missed problems because the handwriting was too messy to read, even by the one who produced it. Anytime my children have to write numbers- dailies, responses, hands-on activities, games, anytime – they are given graph paper to do so. It keeps math neat, readable and makes the math journal a much nicer portfolio to present for evaluation or simply "showing off" to others.

Math Games

Remember what I said in the introduction? That fun learning is easier on the student and the teacher, because making learning fun makes it easier for the student to approach new concepts and understand new things? And that making learning fun makes it easier on the teacher, because the student is so much more receptive and eager to participate, and the learning seems to "stick" longer? Well, maths learning is no exception, and in my experience, is more effective the more fun you can make it. To that end, we use two types of math games – those that are designed to specifically teach or practice math skills and those that simply use math in part of the game experience. And of those, we have two types – purchased and homemade. If you have a deck of cards (even UNO cards will do,) a set of dominoes and a few stray dice around your house somewhere, you have a treasure trove of math games just waiting to be played.

Card Games

Remember the old game of War? Well, it's still a great way to teach and reinforce greater than/less than. Make it more challenging by laying 2 or 3 cards at a time, comparing 2 and 3 digit numbers instead of just one. For older children, you can play rousing games of "Operations War" where all the face cards are removed (keep the aces) to create a deck from 1 – 10. Next, declare the operation that MUST be used – addition, subtraction, multiplication or division – in each round. Then each player lays down 2 cards (3 in the case of division) and performs the necessary operation to see who has the greater hand. You may want to play three cards with subtraction, too, so that instead of 9 – 1, you get 19 – 6. If you end up with a stinker of a division problem, say 17 ÷ 7, allow rounding or estimating, rather than worrying with fractions or remainders. Don't forget Fractions War, where the two cards become the numerator and denominator of a fraction and the two fractions in the round are then compared to determine the winner.

Another great, fun card game to practice basic operations is Computations. Again, remove the face cards, leaving the aces, to create a deck of 1 – 10. (This is why UNO cards work rather well, only they stop at nine.) The players decide on a number target before they begin paying. (My children always choose 27, but that's just us.) The dealer gives each player four cards. Using those four cards and the four basic operations, the players must combine their four numbers to arrive as closely to the target number as possible. For example, if the target is 27, and I'm dealt a 4, 9, 3 and 2, I can do the following: 4 X 9 = 36. 36 – 3 = 33. 33 – 2 = 31. That's difference of 4 and that's my score for that round. The player with the lowest score after 10 rounds wins. We use the sand timer from one of our other games to limit the amount of time players have to make their computations.

For an even greater challenge, play Computations with two decks of cards. The first deck gives you your hand of four numbers. The second deck determines the operations you must use: hearts = addition, spades = subtraction, clubs = multiplication and diamonds = division. You can decide for yourself if you must use the operations in the order they are dealt, or if you are simply limited to using those operations in that hand in any order you choose. Again, lowest score wins the game.

Purchased card games like UNO, SET, Mille Borne, Dutch Blitz, Rack-O, Pit and Crazy Eights also utilize some form of maths in their game play. UNO, Rack-O and Crazy Eights are wonderful for teaching those earliest numeracy skills – comparing, matching, even number identification and numerical order. SET reinforces both logic and set building. Mille Borne uses the disguise of an automobile race to use addition and subtraction as you travel along throughout the race. (There's a good bit of strategy involved, as well.) Dutch Blitz uses numbers, but it is almost strictly a logic or strategy building game, as you must out-think your opponent to win. Pit puts you into the pit at the stock exchange, and is a wonderful way to teach and reinforce money and operations skills, as you trade stocks with the best of them. There's even a series of books and games that use playing cards – from the *Boxcars and One Eyed Jacks* folks – that use playing cards to teach and reinforce various math skills. Deal up some learning on your next game night. The kids may never even know.

Dice Games

Dice are another great source of math game fun. You can use four dice in place of the cards in basic Computations. A child can play a solitaire version of computations easier with dice than with cards, taking ten turns and keeping score just for fun or practice. A random "drill" can be instantly created by simply roiling 2 dice and then performing the called for operation. Roll two dice to create a fraction. Roll again to create another fraction then practice your fraction operations with your two fractions. Explore probability by rolling your dice 10 or 20 times and recording the frequency of the numbers you just rolled. Practice counting skills by racing along a hundreds chart to see who can get to the bottom quickest. Or practice subtracting or negative numbers and race to the top of the chart. Dice can be a fast and easy way to practice all sorts of maths skills.

We practice working with large numbers with a furious game of Pips. For Pips, you need 5 dice. Each 1 rolled is worth 100 points. Each 5 rolled is worth 50 points. A three of a kind is multiplied by 100, while a 4 of a kind is multiplied by 1,000. A roll of Pips – all 5 of a kind at once – scores 10,000 and automatically wins the game. Each player gets three rolls per turn. The first player to reach 10,000 wins.

- EXAMPLE: My first roll is 1, 2, 4, 5 and 6. I keep the 1 and 5. I roll the other three on my second roll. I get a 3 and two 4's. I keep the 4's and roll the remaining die. It's another 4! My score for this turn then is 100 + 400 + 50 = 550. I'm well on my way to 10,000 points with one turn!

For a more challenging game of Pips, declare that only 1's and 5's can be saved, meaning that 3 and 4 of a kinds must be rolled all at once. Now see how easy it isn't to reach 10,000!

Possibly the most well-known dice game is Yahtzee. It is wonderful for practicing multiplication skills, addition skills and strategical thinking. Bunco is another that's gaining popularity, using matching and addition skills. Bunco might be harder to play in a homeschool setting, though as it is a party game requiring teams of players. Don't forget the "boxcars" in the *Boxcars and One Eyed Jacks* books and games. They've come up with ways to use dice to teach and reinforce math that I never would've thought possible.

Domino Games

Dominoes are another wonderful way to add a little fun to your math program. They are automatic fractions for reading, comparing, working problems with. They can also be used for operations practice, performing computations between the halves or between two dominoes. Play a standard game to reinforce number matching and counting skills. Or try your hand at Time Trails.

Times Trails is one of those games I came up with because I needed something new and different for practicing multiplication. The object is to be the player with the highest score by creating multiplication problems as you play. Each player draws 5 dominoes from the pile. The player with the highest double plays first. He places the double and receives the score of the two halves multiplied. He takes a new domino from the pile and play continues to the next player. She must lay any domino containing at least one matching half perpendicular to the first. She multiplies the non-matching half to the double number to receive her score. For example this:

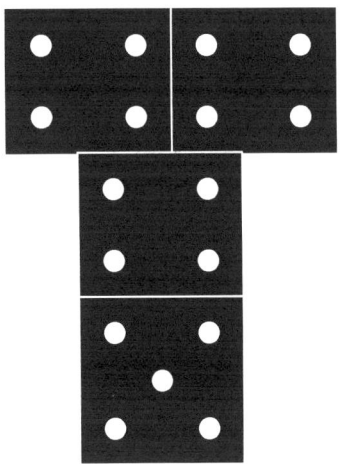

results in Player 1 gaining 16 points from 4 X 4, while player 2 receives 20 points for 4 X 5. If the next player were to lay a 5/2 domino next, he'd have a score of 10 for that hand. (The third player in the example above would have the option of matching with the 5 or with the double 4, increasing his scoring possibilities.) If a player can't play because he has no matching dominoes for any "open" trail, you can either decide he must skip his turn, or that he play draw from the pile until he finds a match. Play continues until someone uses all of his or her dominoes or until no more dominoes can be played by any player and there are no dominoes left to draw.

There are a few domino games books for purchase, outlining various games. The problem I've found with them is that the math skills are often minimal, preferring instead to focus on strategy skills instead. If you really need inspiration, try *Domino Math* and its sequel *More Domino Math*. They may be a bit hard to find, but they will provide you with hours of domino math fun.

Board Games

Many of our favorite and venerated board games reinforce maths skills. You probably have several of them lying around in a closet or cupboard somewhere, overlooked for their math value, relegated to the odd family game night or rainy Saturday afternoon. Pull them out and start working those math muscles. And the kids will definitely not realize this time!

- Strategy/Logic Skills
    - Chess
    - Checkers
    - Othello
    - Sequence
    - SET
    - Rush Hour
    - Pente
    - Mancala
    - Clue
    - Mastermind

- Numeracy Skills

    - Bingo
    - Sorry
    - Chutes and Ladders

- Money Skills
    - Monopoly
    - PayDay
    - Game of Life
    - Settlers of Catan

- Spatial Skills
    - Jigsaw Puzzles

- Graphing
    - Battleship

Fun with Geometry

  There are several ways to cheaply and easily have fun with geometry. Geoboards are great little tools to use to teach shapes, create shapes, and explore angles, tessellations, reflections, rotations, and other concepts, all with a few rubber bands. Tangrams are the ancient Oriental puzzles, created with a set of shapes. There are a whole host of books and websites devoted to the art and play of tangrams. Origami is another fun and artistic way to explore various aspects of geometry, as well as spatial reasoning skills. Again, books, kits and websites are plentiful – check your library, and not just the children's section – for your enjoyment. There's even origami for Christmas so you can decorate the tree and practice your geometry at the same time.

Maths in Motion

  Maths in Motion is what we call the real, living, moving portion of our maths learning. My children don't have to wonder if they'll ever use the math they are learning, or wonder what the fuss over geometry or measurement or fractions is really all about. They'll know because they'll have experienced it as they went along. Once a week or so we take a day and we put our math into practice. We go shopping, both on paper with the weekly advert flyers and to buy the groceries or other necessary items. We take trips, both imaginary ones using our maps, current fuel prices and mileage rates, and real ones in the family car. We cook, doubling, tripling or halving recipes as needed, both as an exercise in using fractions, and to concoct something tasty from the kitchen. We make, build and design things – woodworking projects, quilting and sewing projects, outdoor projects like bird feeders and flower beds. And yes, some are real and some are simply on paper. It doesn't seem to matter whether we actually do the thing, or if it stays on paper, as far as the math is involved. The children enjoy the excitement, if not always the work effort involved, of doing things "for real."

Some suggestions for math in motion activities you might want to consider trying:

- Shopping sprees – Select a budget amount to spend, or a certain number of items that must be bought, or a certain number of guests to feed first. Then, give your child the flyers and catalogs and see what he can come up. I once gave my children the holiday toy catalogs and $300. First, they simply had to spend their $300 in any way they chose. Then, they had to see how few toys could be purchased for $300. Then, they had to supply the toys for a children's Christmas party, where there would be 5 boys and 6 girls. All of the girls would receive the same toys in their stockings and the boys would receive all the same toys, but no toys could be the same between the boys and girls. It kept them busy for an entire afternoon, but they had a lot of fun practicing their math skills that day.

- Cooking – I find cooking is an excellent way to practice all sorts of maths skills. From basic operations to fractions, from measurements to time – working in the kitchen is a very math-intensive experience. Once my daughter started working with fractions, I'd often give her recipes and have her double them, or halve them, or cut them down by a third or fourth. My son has mastered figuring how much time will elapse before something is finished, or what time it will be when the cake is done. And actually cooking with your children can create wonderful memories as well as wonderful learning opportunities.

- Traveling – We've never been to London, England or Adverikie, Scotland, but we know how many miles they are from our house, how long it would take to get there, and how much plane tickets would cost. We've been to the beach, and we figured how much we would need for fuel and food before we left, as well as how many miles and hours we would have to be on the road. We've converted the mileage between home and dance class to kilometers, discussed the proper psi for our tires (alright, perhaps not strictly maths, but it was numbers, right?) and graphed the prices of fuel everyday for a month. And most of that was done without ever leaving the drive.

- Building/Designing – construction, sewing, quilting, gardening, redecorating, and other Do It Yourself pursuits have offered us a plethora of real life math opportunities. And of the myriad of projects we've dreamed up, discussed and designed we've only actually made a fraction of them. My daughter likes to design dresses, and I like to have her figure the cost of the materials or the amount of fabric she'll need to actually sew them up. We've designed hundreds of quilts on paper, but only ever made one. We drew all sorts of designs for gardens and flower beds this spring, but only planted the one we finally agreed would work best. And as for construction and redecorating projects, well if your house is anything like mine, there is always something on the need-to-do list, but only so much time-to-do anything. We have built bird feeders, tables for our family room, shelves for our kitchen and hall closet, repainted every room in the house since we purchased it, planted a very lovely front garden of perennial flowers, built a patio in the back garden and constructed a doll clothing cabinet and a castle-shaped bookcase for a certain little boy's collection of knights and horses, catapults and castles. The next time something needs doing, involve your children, regardless of how young they are. The maths education they'll receive from the experience can't be bought in the most expensive math curriculum.

Putting It All Together

So you've rounded up your games, prepared your math journals, checked a stack of literary math books from the library, and now what? How do you put together a math program that will actually have your children developing and growing? The answer is quite simple, really. Set out your schedule. The average homeschooler "does" school for 32 to 40 weeks. Divide your time into 4 or 5 or 6 terms, whichever works out best. Choose your focus skill families from the list at the beginning of the chapter and assign one to each term. Meet your child where she is – beginning division, 3 digit multiplication, addition with carrying over – and begin from there. Meanwhile, use your dailies to keep those old skills fresh and sharp. Use your games, books and brain teasers, along with your manipulatives to do your teaching and practicing. A typical week down my son's living math path might look something like this:

1. Monday – Using manipulatives to create the six times tables. Daily sheet of 8 addition problems utilizing carrying over.
2. Tuesday – A game of Times Trails, using our double 6 set of dominoes. Daily sheet of 8 subtraction problems using borrowing.
3. Wednesday – A "Math in Motion" activity involving feeding the family of four fro the weekly market flyers. He has to figure up the costs involved in purchasing 4 of everything. (At this stage, I allow rounding so that he's only working with single digit numbers.) His daily page that day has 10 problems, a mix of subtraction and addition.
4. Thursday – Free Math – Choosing an activity from our "math box" of manipulatives or our shelf of math puzzle books. After three days of hard work on his multiplication, having a day of something fun and most likely NOT multiplication-related is a welcome break. Daily page of 6 word problems using subtraction and addition.
5. Friday – Family Math Day – We'll all sit down and play a few games, most probably Combinations or Yahtzee or something that DOES involve multiplying, but perhaps something that focuses on his sister's geometry skills instead. Or, if there's enough time and I'm not begged for "just one more game" we might play games for both.

His math journal for the week will have his 4 dailies entered in. The pages he created using his rods on Monday will be placed in the Hands-On section. His paper from Wednesday will go in responses. If he made a paper on Thursday, that will be filed appropriately. If not, he'll fill out two math activity pages (you can find a sample one in the Appendix) – one for his Free Math and one for Family Math on Friday.

Conclusion

Teaching maths doesn't need to be scary, for either the teacher or the student. It needn't be dry, dull, drill-filled drudgery. Maths can come alive through good books, games, hands-on activities and real-life applications. Purchasing math manipulatives and the resource books to teach you how to use them (or teach your children by using them) can be an expensive investment, but it can be done over time, and many of those manipulatives and tools can be used all the way through to high school. Think of all the money you'll spend by *not* purchasing math curriculum year in and year out, too, and compare it to the relatively low cost of manipulatives and resource books. It becomes a bit more bearable, doesn't it? Living maths creates learners who not only know their mathematical skills and concepts, but how to use them in real life. That's our ultimate goal, isn't Math Wimps, to create Math Machos confident in their skills and bold in their abilities? So, no more Math Wimps allowed!!

∞ ∞ ∞

SOCIAL STUDIES

What IS Social Studies, Anyway?

Social studies is that rather broad term encompassing history, geography, cultural awareness and citizenship. History tells us of the great deeds of great men and women, helps us to place ourselves in the great river of time, and builds for us a foundation for the future. Geography shows us our place among the rest of the world, labels our world with boundaries both natural and man-made, and leads us home and to lands far away. Cultural awareness helps us to see that for all of our differences, we are all fundamentally alike in greater and more numerous ways than we are not. The knowledge necessary to make future citizens of our children – the fundamental frameworks of government, economics, and patriotism – prepare our children to take their future places in society with confidence and competence. Social studies, therefore, is just as much about the future as it is about the past. I love the illustration on the title page of this chapter. The little ones reaching forward for their globe as it rests upon their open book exemplifies to me this past and future intertwined – the young reaching forward happily for the world and its already-recorded stories. That's the sort of thing I'd like to think I'm instilling in my children when it comes to social studies.

What Do I Need?

All that is truly needed to teach social studies are a timeline of some sort; atlases, globes and or maps; a three-ring binder with paper, and quality literature. Timelines can consist of large wall-mounted chronologies made of sheets of paper connected together end-to-end, or individual smaller notebook bound "book of centuries" for each student. Notebooks are used to house lists – vocabulary; kings, queens, presidents, and other rulers; discoveries and explorers; scientists; inventions – you name it. Atlases, globes and maps should be up-to-date and appropriate to a student's age and abilities. This means that they should change over the years, gradually becoming more complex and "complete" as the student and her studies mature. Literature selections should include both fiction and non-fiction, modern and classic. Biographies, autobiographies, historical fiction, travel guides, picture books, cookbooks, magazines, even the daily newspaper fit the bill for social studies studying. Anything that discusses other places, other times, memorable events or people in a literary, interesting and age-appropriate manner will find itself useful in teaching social studies.

Using Literature

There are two ways to go about teaching social studies using literature. The first is to simply use whatever you have on hand, and the second is to carefully select certain titles for the historical, geographical, or cultural elements they contain.

Nearly any and every title contains some elements useful for social studies instruction. Even science fiction, fantasy and fairy tales deal with human interactions, make use of cultural, economic, or civic conventions (or the lack of them) and are therefore very appropriate for discussions on and instruction in those matters. So, while your children's favorite storybook may not, at first glance have much to offer, looking at it with the eyes of a social studies teacher may give it a whole new place in your lesson planning. Let's take for an example Beatrix Potter's international favorite "The Tale of Peter Rabbit,"

On the surface, it's a lovely little story about the misadventures of a naughty little bunny boy. Examine it a little deeper and you'll find a treasure trove of historical, geographical and cultural concepts waiting to be explored and examined. For history lessons, it offers us the Victorian era. How about the role of women in Victorian times for your older student? Or perhaps your science driven technology nut would prefer to study the agricultural developments and innovations of the Victorian period? The geography of England/Great Britain/the United Kingdom is a must, regardless of age or ability. Simply finding it on the map or globe will suffice for the youngest learners, while the oldest students could be asked to write a report or create a presentation on physical and human geographical features of the country. Would famous women artists and authors of the Victorian period be considered history or culture, do you think? (Does it matter?) Make a list, compare works, read some biographies and explore the lives and works of some inspiring women. Let's not forget, too, the citizenship lessons entwined throughout the story – obeying rules, respect for others' property, going to market, caring for our things (Peter loses his new coat and shoes, after all,) encouraging others to do their best (as the birds did for Peter when he was caught in the netting) and even the role parents play in the health and well-being of their children - can all be found in Peter's sweet little story. Now, are you starting to see Peter Rabbit through the eyes of a social studies teacher? It's a whole new way of looking at and reading literature and periodicals that begins to come naturally after a while.

I mentioned using the daily newspaper a bit ago as a source of social studies material. As you or your older students read the day's stories, make note of the places and events reported upon. Begin a daily habit of finding the locations in your atlas or on your globe. Use current events as springboards for discussions and learning about similar historical or cultural happenings. Politically motivated or generated stories can lead to discussions and lessons in citizenship, patriotism and government. Some economic education will be necessary for the understanding of news from the financial and business world. If a natural or man-made disaster brings one location to attention day after day, use it as an opportunity to spark an in-depth study of the city, country or entire region. Don't forget the human element, too, by studying the culture -- religion, music, food and customs – of those affected. Remember, a living education uses *LIFE*, even the bad, sad, tragic parts of it. Using the daily newspaper to teach our children is one way we can turn tragedy into triumph.

For those who prefer more planning and less spontaneity, you can choose titles that are specific to your goals. Do you want to concentrate on the geography of Asia? Choose titles set on that continent. Is the French Revolution on your list of historical events for this term? Don't forget to read *The Scarlet Pimpernel* then! Nearly every significant event and individual since the dawn of time, including the dawn of time, has been written about at some point, and often for young readers' enjoyment or enlightenment. Your choices for reading material, therefore, are nearly endless.

Social studies is one area where I haven't completely discounted textbooks as reading material, either. Many older, and a few modern history and geography textbooks read much more like novels than the dumbed-down, dried up texts of today, especially those written prior to World War II. They have a literary quality about them, as in they were specifically written to excite the young reader about the topic at hand. While the geography in many of them is no longer accurate as borders and even country's names have changed since they were written, the historical events and individuals they present are still locked away, frozen in time. Often available as reprints or even free for reading and printing online, their engaging tales are just as interesting and entertaining as they were 50 or 100 years ago. They serve well as "spines" – books to hang the rest of our readings on – because they can fill in any gaps our reading might miss, or might not provide opportunities to study. I highly recommend spine texts when studying history with young children, especially, because it can be difficult to find age-appropriate materials to cover many topics.

In addition to literature and my atlases, I like to have some general resources on hand, as well. While they aren't necessary to have, they can add so much color and context to our studies. I find a good history encyclopedia – full of photos, drawings and maps – invaluable to let the student *see* the history he's reading about. It can help to fill in any gaps your reading selections may not cover, as not even all spine texts cover everything you may need or want to know. It can also answer the quick question, like who was the King of England during the American Revolution or what year did the first automobile appear. It can even spark a study into a particular figure or era or event, as a child takes an interest in one of its shorter entries and wants to know more. Among my other resources is a cookbook with recipes from all over the world. While it may be difficult to prepare all the recipes as ingredients may not necessarily be available in my grocery store, there's nothing like a taste of Thailand or a bite of Berlin to add spark to a geography lesson. I have a book that discusses holidays and festivals around the globe, too. Its photos, descriptions and recipes have helped us to understand other cultures better, and to marvel at how all of us seem to have a need to celebrate the passing of time, significant events of human life, and traditions passed down from long-forgotten ancestors. If you can't locate or afford similar resources, don't worry about. As I said, resources other than maps, globes and/or atlases aren't necessary. They are nice to have if you can get them, but you can still teach social studies without them.

Don't forget that history readings, regardless coming from a spine, a selection or a resource book, should be concluded with the occasional narration. As I explained in the language arts chapter, narration is one of the best ways to check for comprehension. How often you include history reading narrations is completely up to you, of course, but once a week or so should be enough to check and make sure your child understands who, what and when you are studying. I like to include a narration especially after reading about a particularly important person or event. That way, I know that what's most important for my children to know is actually being learned, and that we'll not have to come back at a later point and review or clarify something that was missed the first time.

What's Most Important

There's a debate among homeschoolers as to whether or not history should be taught chronologically. Personally, I don't think it really matters one way or the other, especially to young children. If you use a timeline in conjunction with your history studies, the chronological order of things will become evident as you create it as entries to the timeline are added. Some will argue that isn't enough – the timeline should be filled in from the beginning. Others might say that ancient history should only be studied once a child's religious faith has been firmly established, to avoid confusion or concern over the many and varied gods of the ancient peoples. As I said, I don't think it really matters. Chronological teaching of history isn't the most important thing when dealing with young children and social studies.

Young children, to age 8 or 9, need a firm grasp on their own culture, history and geography. They need to understand some basic principles of patriotism and citizenship, too. This helps them to develop a working understanding of the people, places, events and celebrations that impact their daily lives. Understanding *why* a holiday is observed is more important than *when* the event being commemorated first took place. Knowing *what* and *why* the national flag looks as it does is more useful to a young child than knowing *when* it was created or by *whom*. Grasping *who* is honored with the statue or plaque or portrait and *why* they are so honored is much more meaningful than *when* that individual lived. Understanding which war Grandpa is a veteran of is more important than knowing *when* it was fought. Recognizing that their country has a president or a prime minister or a queen and that makes it different from a country without one is more useful than knowing *who* that person is or *where* they live. Learning what makes their family, their town, their country different, special and unique from all the others in the world helps young children develop a sense of understanding of their place, their time, their rituals – their lives. Therefore, if your children are younger, start small, start local, begin with the familiar. Give your children a firm foundation of relevant living history, geography, culture and citizenship on which to build their future studies.

A great deal of beginning history can be taught through family stories and field trips to familiar places. Think about it – your family doesn't exist in a time vacuum. Grandpa served his country proudly, and your child should hear why and how he served. The town square has a statue of a famous general or statesman. He's certainly important to the history and culture of your area. The history museum has a room of toys and games and other recreations from the past – just the perfect thing to introduce your children to the lives and times that came before them! Geography is all around you, too. Just look out your window and marvel at the sun setting in the west, or the stars above you. The road signs point the way north along the river, while the way to grandma's house leads south. You live in a county that is part of a state that is part of a country that is part of continent that is part of this big, wide world around you. The ocean is east of you and the mountains are to the west. Your family is Irish or Cuban or Italian or Scottish or Native. You're Catholic or Protestant or Hindu or Muslim. Your town was founded 500 years ago or 50 or 5. The post office displays the national flag, while city hall flies the state and municipal banners, too. The fire department is important to the safety of our community. Local, relevant history, geography, culture and citizenship concepts are all around you. Take advantage of them and introduce your young children to the things that matter most in their lives.

Using Timelines

I prefer a notebook timeline, or book of centuries, for our timelines. Some families create a large wall-mounted timeline, taping together long sheets of poster board or paper to create it. Others take that same long stretch of timeline, fold it up and fasten one end into a binder or notebook, thus combining the two principles – a long flow of history with a convenient storage system. I like notebooks because so much can be added to them. We have maps, coloring pages, drawings, illustrations, stories and narrations, games and puzzle sheets – you name it, we've probably put it into our timeline notebooks at some point! A timeline doesn't have to be anything fancy or formal. You create it as you go along with your readings and studies. It is simply a chronological record of all the people and events you've learned about in your travels.

How you divide history (and therefore your timeline) is also up to you. A true book of centuries is just that – it is made up of one century spans per page or double page layout. We tried this traditional timeline format when we first began, and I didn't really like using it. For one thing, there's only so much room for entries, even on a double page configuration. I think a true book of centuries' format is fine if you are studying rulers, or developments in science, or the history of music or some other smaller facet of time. For a general, broad overview of history, it's not so great, if you ask me. For one thing, what do you do with someone born in one century and then has the nerve to die in the next? Where do they go? And how do you denote something like the 100 Years' War, which lasted a very long time indeed? I much prefer to borrow a page from the Classical homeschoolers and divide history up into 4 eras – Ancient (pre-500AD,) Medieval (500 - 1500,) Renaissance (1500 – 1850,) and Modern (1850 to present day.) (Now, you may not think 1850 is exactly "modern" but if you look at the philosophies, diets, work habits and lifestyles of folks in the 1850's and now, you'll see that they have more in common with us than they did with the folks of even 50 years earlier.) So, we've divided our timelines into 4 parts and simply file entries in order as we encounter them. As to what to do with those pesky folks born in one century and dying in another, well, you have a choice here in our home school – either place their page by birth or by death. As to those *really* pesky individuals who are born in one *era* and then proceed to live into another, we simply mark both their birth *and* their death (and usually an achievement or two along the way, as well.)

I purchased our timeline template years ago and it still serves us well. You really don't need a fancy template or purchased timeline, though. Create yours with blank paper and art supplies. Just remember to mark the year, at least, at the top of each page before you file it away. (Our timeline pages have a little box in the upper right-hand corner for placing the date(s) which makes it easy when you want to find where your latest page should fit in.) Devote each page to a person or event. Read about the person, or watch a documentary about an event, or simply discuss who that fellow is wearing the funny looking clothes in the statue on the town square and then draw a picture of him on your page. You can also include clippings from magazines and/or newspapers, printouts from a computer, even postage stamps depicting famous people or events or a photo of that funny looking fellow from the square. Then, somewhere on the page, write a sentence or two or an entire narration based on your reading and studying, explaining who or what your page is about. File it in its proper place and you've just made history! There's a sample timeline page in the Appendix, but it is a bare sample, nothing more, just to give you an idea of how to start.

History

History is the journey through time. It is how we arrived at where we are, and who it was that went before and blazed the trails. It is a living, flowing thing. History was 5,000 years ago. It was 5 years ago, 5 minutes ago, 5 seconds ago. History is the story from the road down which Life has come, and is continuing to go. Without it, we are doomed to get lost – taking a wrong turn for lack of experience – or spend too much time looking for a path because we didn't pay attention to the road markers. The way our children perceive history is much different than the way we see it, too. For us, a year is one 30th or one 40th of our lifespan – a drop in the bucket in our river of Life. But to a 9 year old, a year is one 9th of his lifespan – a rather sizable chunk of his time in existence. He also has fewer reference points, too. We have 30 or 40 or more birthdays, spring times, summers, autumns and winters to look back upon. He has 5 or 6 that he can clearly remember, maybe one or two more for which he has some vague recollection. We must understand this if we are going to impart a true sense of history to our children, especially when they are very young.

When beginning history with young children, start at the end, not the beginning. Begin their timeline with the current year. Have them draw a self-portrait or paste a current photo. Then work backward slowly, chronicling their birthdays, birthdays of younger siblings, and other significant events in their short lives, until you reach their births. Then, next add the births of any older siblings, perhaps your marriage, your birth and other important events from your lifetime. Go back one more generation, to include grandparents' weddings, births, etc. This helps your young child to see where he fits into this thing called "time" and "history." It also gives him some reference points when he hears family stories, or learns about important events. (He won't make mistakes like my son did when he asked my Baby Boomer mother what it was like living through the Great Depression.) Starting his timeline at the "end" will help him see, later on when he begins to study history outside of his own family time span, just how long ago Genghis Khan lived, and that space travel really is a relatively "new" thing. Older children can benefit from this backward timeline process, too. Helping them assemble a timeline of their lifetimes and that of their parents can help them to understand that not all of history was made centuries ago and that modern history has many important events they might not have studied or read about simply by virtue of their being so new.

Once your child is ready for "real" history, again I advise starting locally, sort of – with your country's past. Young children need to know the important dates and individuals that helped to shape the country into what it has become today. If you aren't certain who to begin with, take a look at a calendar, at the monuments that have been constructed, and at the events and people still being presented in books, documentaries and such. If someone is considered highly enough to have been granted a commemorative holiday or statue, then they are necessary to your child's education, because they are necessary for living in your society. Likewise, events that are worthy of national remembrance are essential to your child's cultural knowledge. Imagine an American child not knowing the significance of July Fourth, or a British student ignorant of Guy Fawkes! How much detail you discuss is going to depend on your child's age and maturity level. A 4 year old simply needs to know that Guy Fawkes tried and failed to blow up Parliament and the King. An 8 year old is capable of doing a multi-week unit study of the American Revolution, including July 4th and the Declaration of Independence. A 12 year old can do an in-depth study of John Adams or Thomas Jefferson or King James I.

After spending a year or two or even three covering your nation's history, you'll want to look both outward and inward with your history focus. Looking outwardly, you'll want to begin studying world history. If you don't agree with teaching ancient history, with its pantheons of gods and mythologies, to young children then taking the time to teach your children their national history will allow you some years for rooting them in their own faith, so as not to confuse or concern them. If you believe that world history should be taught from the start, let me assure you that children are quite capable of learning both world and national history at the same time. Using your timeline helps clear up any confusion that might arise from studying two different time periods, and if you schedule your history so as to make it certain to your students which is which, they'll have no troubles keeping the two studies apart. (We schedule "local" history for certain days each week, and world history on others, even though my children are well past the age of becoming confused.) Looking inwardly, it's now time to reduce your history focus to your state, province or region. Every child needs to have a good working understanding of their home region and its history. One way of beginning a study of "local" history is to start with your family tree. You've already begun a brief history of your family through your initial timeline studies. Add to this by including more distant relatives and more events. Cast your nets even further to bring in more history. Another option is to start with an event important to your locale. We're not that far from sites significant to both the French and Indian War, and the American Civil War. So, naturally, our study of local history began with these two events and then we worked our way forward and backward to include the entire span of our state's history. Again, by making the students aware that they are studying a different time period for a different reason and for a specific region helped to keep their world and local history separate.

One added benefit of studying the history of more than one region is that children can sometimes make connections between the two, especially when using a timeline. *Oh, the French and Indian War was part of the Seven Years War..... Hey, Victoria was Queen during the American Civil War!* These associations may not be as easily spotted with mere reading alone. The fact that an entry about Victoria's husband Albert's death is right after the entry on the First Battle of Bull Run makes it almost impossible to miss the link between the two.

The basics of your history studies will, of course, be your literature selections and your timelines, but don't forget to bring your history study alive with activities and memorable moments. Find and try some recipes from your historical era. Explore the fashions of the day, too, with costumes or paper dolls. Visit places of importance, especially if re-creations or re-enactments are involved. Living museums are wonderful resources for literally bringing history alive before your eyes. Watch historical movies or documentaries. Learn a craft or skill useful to people living then. Play a game or two popular with children of the time. Listen to some of the era's music, perhaps even learn to sing or play a tune or two. Remember, the people of the day didn't just write great books or fight fierce battles. They ate, they drank, they sang, they played, they read, and they dressed in the latest styles their income could afford. In short they *lived.* Your children will remember more about them and their place in time if they too can *live* a little of their lives, as well. These opportunities to bring history to life and to add life to your studies will leave your children with an enduring enjoyment of history, as well as memorable moments spent in living education.

Geography

Not to sound like a broken record, but when beginning the study of geography, you should start with your small child's small world. One of my children's first geography lessons was to make a map of their own bedroom. They learned east and west in the front yard watching the sunsets. North and south were taught while trying to find the Big Dipper. We've planned together trips to grandpa's house and to summer camp, following along on the maps as we've traveled. They learned the names of local landforms by simply talking about them. *We go up the hill to get to town. We live near the river. The park is on a small peninsula in the river.* Children in Arizona are going to learn the landforms of the desert, while children in the city will learn the language of street signs and road markings. Just as our children live within the river of time, they are surrounded by the landscape of geography. Use what's at hand. It will interest them most, and serve them best in the future.

There are really three parts to geography, and all are important in your child's education. Physical geography is the actual, natural land around us. The hills, rivers, lakes, mountains, plains, deserts, oceans and ice fields that surround us are our physical geography. We've given name and labels to these features of our world, but we neither created them nor can we completely obliterate them. Political geography is the way in which we humans have divided the natural world around us. Borders and boundaries mark our world into ever increasingly smaller bits. From continents, to countries, to regions, provinces, states, counties, parishes, townships, cities, towns, villages, farms, fields, neighborhoods, and finally to plots and lots –

we've carved the land and water up and given them names and boundaries that denote ownership. Human geography is the way in which we use our lands and waters. We grow grain here and raise cattle there. We forest here and fish there. A child has to know the names and features of physical geography, the names and locations of political geography, and the human nature of the natural world in order to best understand just what this "world" is, and where his place in it lies.

For physical geography, start with the landforms and climates around you. It will come naturally, in a way, as you explain the physical features of your child's world in your day-to-day interactions. You can study the weather and learn about your local climate. Make a list or drawings for your notebook identifying the various features of the landscape in which you live. If you travel, take the opportunity to add the features of your temporary world to your knowledge bank, too. When you're ready to add more, study the physical features of your favorite books or movies. Or better yet, read books and watch movies for their scenery and surroundings. Revel in Andrew Lang's *Arabian Nights* and study the great deserts of the world. Travel to the frozen North with Balto or White Fang. Visit the rolling Midlands of England with our old friend, Peter Rabbit. Head to the seashore with Pagoo, or find the Great Barrier Reef with Nemo. There's a beautiful, fascinating wide world out there. Discover it!

Political geography can begin with simple exercises in daily life – learning your home address; finding your home country on an atlas or globe; discovering which states border yours; which country lies to the south or north, which to the east and west. What's the name of your capital city? The largest city nearby? Move up to a more systematic study of the states in your region, or the countries of Europe or North America. Start local and work outwardly, eventually encompassing the entire world. Learn the names of states, provinces, counties, countries and their capitals, continents and their countries. Don't forget the rivers and lakes, seas and oceans, too. In physical geography, you've learned what makes a lake a lake and a mountain a mountain. In political geography, you'll learn what the name of that lake is, and which river flows through Paris. Your literature selections can help with this, of course, as can your atlas or globe. Don't require memorization of the facts, much. Go for recognition instead. The political nature of the world is both permanent and fluid at the same time. The city of Prague has been central to the Czech people for nearly 1100 years, but the river which flows through it bears two separate and recognized names, and the country which it governs is less than 20 years old. Fluid, yet unchanging, yes?

Human geography is even more fluid than political geography. Human geography is the study of the ways in which man uses the land he inhabits. Economics, agriculture, tourism, education and government all play a part in human geography. Culture and climate have their say, as well. What do the farmers in your area grow? How are the streets marked? Do you live in an urban or rural environment? How has the weather affected your area lately? Drought? Floods? Too much snow or too hot a summer? Human geography also concerns itself with movements of people – immigration, migration, emigration – why are they leaving or arriving, and where are they coming from and going to? It is, perhaps, the least important type of geography for our students, at least at the ages we're dealing with here. It would be enough to know that Kansas is a great supplier of wheat, or that in Appalachia coal is a big economic factor. Urban sprawl and natural disasters like floods and droughts are often the effects of Man's mismanagement of the land and waters. Our children need to be aware of these things, too. Again, strive for recognition, rather than memorization. There's time later to learn the main products of Spain or the spread of the Influenza epidemic. For now, knowing ways in which we humans impact our world, both good and bad, are enough.

Atlas Quests

One fun and free way that we study geography is through atlas quests. Think of a quest as a scavenger hunt with an atlas. I'll go through the atlas and write down 5 or 6 questions for the children to discover the answers to. Some samples:

- What is the name of the river that flows through New York City?
- Find two straits. What are their names? Where are they located?
- What is the capital city of Massachusetts?
- What countries in Africa are crossed by the equator?
- Locate 3 deserts. What countries are they in?

- Trace the borders of the country directly north of Paraguay. Label it and its capital city.

Some atlas quest pages are simply a list of the letters of the alphabet down the page, with instructions to find a city for each letter. Or contain a list of cities, rivers, etc. with instructions to find the country that contains them all. Others might have a country traced out, and ask the student to find it, name the country, and mark and label the capital city. Some are location specific – with questions all centered in a state or region or country. A few are just a jumble of questions whose answers may be found anywhere between the covers of the atlas. Sometimes, we'll do a literary quest, where I ask them to find countries or cities named in our recent readings. Every now and then we do an "artsy" quest, in which the answers are flags of countries or states, or the state trees or flowers shown in our US atlas. In place of merely writing the answer, the children have to draw the required flag or flower or tree. The possibilities for quests are nearly endless. The only limitations are your children's abilities, your atlas's information, and your imagination in creating the quest pages.

We have a world atlas and a US atlas. I prefer the *National Geographic Atlases for Young Explorers*, but any good age-appropriate atlas will work. Most times I'm nice and let them know which atlas contains the answers. Other times I'm not and just let them hunt their way through both until they find their answers. When they were younger, I always told them. Now that they're older, I find they learn more through longer, more involved questing. The questing nature of the activity keeps the learning fresh and exciting, while the often open-ended questions mean that learning is not confined to right or wrong. My children have learned more in an afternoon of atlas questing than they ever did using formal geography lessons. Did you know that China is an excellent source of cities whose names begin with the letters X and Q? They do, but they learned that through questing, not through worksheets or textbooks that told them so. Obtain a good atlas or two, and quest your way to painless, fun geography learning! There are a few sample atlas quest questions in the Appendix that would work with any atlas, for those of you who're ready for your own questing.

Cultural Awareness

The public schools are often admonished for their insistence on teaching "multiculturalism" over "domestic culture," but that doesn't mean that our children can't or shouldn't learn about cultures other than their own. It simply means that there needs to be a balance and a proper attitude towards the subject. Young children tend to see other cultures as exotic and exciting, yet thrill to learn of the similarities they share with these "otherworldly" people. Older children and students are often fascinated with those very same similarities – a child their own age in a country far away can enjoy the same pastimes, study the same subjects in school, and celebrate similar holidays – how can that *be*? Older children are also more receptive to the magical differences of others' ways of life – different foods, strange languages, colorful festivals, new traditions, old customs – all just waiting to be discovered and experienced. Bringing a bit of the world into our little corner of it makes it both a bigger world, with many more people and ways of living than our children ever imagined, and a smaller one, with our many similarities drawing us closer than our differences keep us apart.

There are many opportunities to explore the richness of other cultures in homeschooling without great expense. As we already saw with our friend Peter Rabbit, simply exploring the culture in which a story is set is one way to go about it. Another is to plan a deliberate study, choosing readings and activities meant to explore a country, continent or culture. A third is to take advantage of an event like the Olympics, a missionary speaker, a trip or travel opportunity, or a current news happening to determine which culture or country to investigate. There's a seemingly endless realm of possibilities for ideas to delve into other lands and cultures.

Whatever the origin of your study, it's best to begin with your atlas, globe or map. Knowing the physical location of your chosen country or region is the first step. Your younger children can see just how near or far away you are from it, while your older children can place it among the "known" locations already in their store of knowledge. You'll be surprised, too, at how much geography your children will remember with relative ease when it's been placed in respect to its people, language, customs, etc. as well as in relation to your reading, event or planned "itinerary." After you've established the physical location of your destination, move on into general aspects of the culture. Topics like the language and unique foods may be enough of an introduction for your youngest students. Showing pictures or video of native dress and/or dance, listening to ethnic music and learning a bit about religion or holidays, in addition to language and food, will suffice for older students. Your oldest students may want to explore the history, economy or political nature of your destination as well, especially if something is relevant to a current event such as a war, disaster or celebration. You can use stories, encyclopedias, documentary films, magazines and newspapers, even travel brochures and guides as sources of information. There are coloring books and paper dolls showing ethnic dress for many cultures. Libraries often have foreign language materials both for reading and for learning the language that you can use. Look for authentic recipes too, in cookbooks, magazines and even online. The best possible source of learning would be someone who has lived in or is a part of that culture, for they can give first hand experiences and knowledge that even the best book or travel film can't impart.

Be Careful With Others' Cultures, Please

I feel I should give a few words of caution here. America, Canada, Australia and even the United Kingdom are nations of immigrants. We should take care not to confuse "immigrant" customs surrounding us with authentic "native" customs. One good example of this is the fact that many Irish and Canadian Americans celebrate St. Patrick's Day with a meal of corned beef and cabbage. In Ireland, it is more traditional to have lamb or mutton, roasted or stewed. Corned beef was more readily available in the Irish immigrant neighborhoods of the 19th century, and therefore became a "new" tradition. Australians have similar immigrant traditions, such as Christmas barbecues, that the original settlers began to replace holiday customs difficult to carry on in their new home. When studying a particular culture, it is easy to imagine that these immigrant customs we're familiar with were simply transplanted from the "old country" and confuse them with authentic traditional customs.

We should take care, too, not to present the cultures of others as something of a curiosity or as "quaint" traditions. It is natural for our children to see the strange dress and foods of Africa's tribal people as something "cute" or "funny" when in reality it is simply a matter of everyday life for them. We need to remind our children to respect the ways of others, and not to make fun of them or belittle them.

It is likewise easy to make judgments based on differences of religion, politics or customs. Just because a South American child living in the Amazon doesn't wear much clothing doesn't mean she's too poor to do so. It's probably more due to the fact that her tropical climate makes wearing a great deal of clothing physically uncomfortable. When a Hindu child paints himself and others with many colors for the festival of Holi, it is an act of worship and celebration and should be viewed as such, and not as some "heathen" tradition or "pagan" belief anymore than a Christian child's dyeing of Easter eggs or singing of Christmas carols. We all live our lives in our own ways. We're different. Different isn't wrong, and our children need to learn that. They will have to share their lives and their world with an ever-increasing number of those they might view as different. Bias or discrimination based solely on cultural differences can be damaging to their future. Use differences as teaching tools to point out your customs, beliefs and traditions if you must. Don't use them to form harmful judgments or prejudices, please.

Citizenship

Citizenship is a rather broad term for the concepts and ideas that your children need to know in order to take their place as informed citizens of their respective country. Patriotism, economics, political structures, laws, rights and responsibilities – all make up the knowledge vital to active, productive citizenship. In short, it is those things that one must know, or at least be familiar with, in order to successfully function in the society of one's native (or adopted) homeland.

Patriotism

Patriotism consists of those things – people, places, events, symbols – which are unique to a country, and which have helped to form its national identity. For younger children, recognizing the flag, learning the national anthem, learning the name and location of the national capital city, great national heroes and leaders, and two or three pivotal events in the nation's history are enough. Many of these people and events will comprise their early history lessons, so you'll be killing two birds with one stone. Older students will want to expand on this base knowledge with national symbols, currency, more people and more events. Again, many of the characters and incidents will be met in their national history studies, and often history studies will lead naturally into citizenship lessons. What American child can truly study the War of 1812 without learning of Francis Scott Key and the American national anthem? Could a British student really study King John and not be introduced to the Magna Charta along the way or vice versa? There are people and incidents from every country that are on equal footing with these. Their historical presence is too strong to ignore.

When it comes to important documents like your national constitution, the Declaration of Independence or the above mentioned Magna Charta, younger students merely need to know their significance in the life of their country. Older students may want to use portions of them as copy work or as sources for memorization. Your oldest student should study the document itself, as well as its writers and signers, and know exactly why it was written, what significance it played in history, and what affects it is still having today. These are the papers, the words that have formed and shaped our nations and our world. A simple passing review is probably not enough to prepare your child for active, responsible citizenship.

Economics

The first economic lesson many children receive is in the form of a coin or piece of paper currency that is all theirs for the first time by right, gift or discovery. They learn its worth, its design, and its symbols. Given the opportunity to spend that money, they receive their second lesson – economics in action. Depending on what it is they wish to purchase, they may receive additional lessons in savings, deficits, borrowing or budgeting. As with all their other lessons, everyday life sets the learning stage with little or no effort from the parent-teacher.

Further economic lessons can be "found" in the pantry cupboard at home. Not only can the cans and boxes be used to play "store" with real or pretend money, but the processes through which the food items have traveled to reach your pantry can be explored. Some farmer had to grow the apples in the juice, while some manufacturer had to run the factory that bottled the juice. A supplier had to sell that juice to the store, where the manager used it to stock his shelves, where you and your family purchased it. Whether the farm, factory and store were independently or government-owned depends on the form of market in place, but the process is there for the exploration regardless. Childhood "play pretends" like store and restaurant are perfect springboards for economic learning. You and your children can learn how to make change, buy on a budget, buy on credit, write a check, place and fill an order, make substitutions for unavailable products, figure discounts and many more basic and not so basic financial concepts. All you need is a little imagination and a few items from pantry or cupboard.

Older children will need to learn the various world and historical economic models. Feudalism, ancient bartering, America's "New Deal" of the 1930's, colonial economies, and other historical economic systems are as important to understanding the shape of today's economic world as they were to the times in which they were in place. Today's global economy is actually a patchwork of various forms of free market and command systems, so in order to fully understand and appreciate the current (and future) state of affairs, our children need to have a working knowledge of economies outside of their own.

Don't forget the entrepreneurial side of things, too. There are quite a few good books for those who might like to try their hand at creating and running their own business. There's even a business math program available for the elementary set. There's nothing like hands-on learning to let them see the realities and simplicities of an otherwise complex and possibly confusing topic.

Government and Law

I've combined government and law because you can't really have one without the other. Government structures make up the legal system, and without laws and rulings, there is usually no stable state government. The two go hand in hand, and our future citizens need to know as much about them as they can.

Young children begin learning about government and laws as soon as they hear a parent say, "No." Families cannot function without rules and a governing structure anymore than society can. You can use your own family structure and "house rules" as examples of caring, responsible government. Out and about in your neighborhood you'll encounter your first civic government examples, in the forms of street signs; police and other emergency services; civil services like libraries, roads, public transit; and parks and other recreational facilities. You are surrounded by both domestic and civil governments. They form the very fabric of society. Your children are surrounded by them, too. Take advantage of as many of them as you can to begin your child's civic education.

Older children can be introduced to the form of national government under which they live. Again, some of this may be a natural extension of history and patriotism lessons, as the topics tend to overlap. Later, once they have a handle on their own country's government structure, they can learn about the governing structures of other nations. It is somewhat easier to learn about different forms of government through comparison, once one way of ruling a country is understood. *Socialism is different from democracy because…..Constitutional monarchism isn't a true monarchy because…..* By having a foundation to hang all the rest on, you make learning the individual forms and relating them to each other and to real-life countries much easier to do.

Your own government is the best source of citizenship information for your oldest students. Request the information necessary for immigrants to become citizens. If your country thinks those wishing to become its newest citizens need to know it, then it would only make sense that your children, as future citizens, need to know it as well.

Hands on experiences always add to learning, and civics is no exception. Attend a town meeting. Take an active part in a local election or debate. Visit your public offices and buildings, if possible. Send public officials a letter of support or concern. Keep a scrapbook of newspaper clippings concerning an issue of public, and personal, concern. Give your children enough information to understand any proceedings they might witness, and the significances of any places they might visit, but not so much that there is nothing left for them to learn through the experience.

Growing future citizens should be one of every parent's goals for his or her children. Complacency through ignorance on the part of its citizens often leads to corruption and domination by an uncontrolled government. Rights only come through responsibility and responsible exercise of those rights.

Your Social Studies Notebook

Like your timeline, your notebook will be an ever-growing, ever-changing portion of your social studies learning. One simple way to set it up, at least in the beginning, is by topic – Geography, Patriotism, Government, Culture, etc. You can be as specific or as general as you like, as notebooking is almost organic, changing as its owner changes. In your notebook, you should put lists, drawings, maps, printouts, copywork, and anything else that pertains to your learning that isn't fodder for your timeline. Here are some suggestions:

- Lists –
  - Presidents, kings, queens and other rulers
  - Landforms
  - Countries within an empire or international pact like NATO
  - Allies in a war
  - Scientists and their inventions/discoveries
  - Explorers and their discoveries
  - Artists and composers of a certain era
  - Cultural aspects of a certain time period
  - Holidays of a certain country or religion
  - Calendars of holidays for a particular year of study
  - Languages spoken by the people of a country, region or continent
  - Vocabulary lists – holidays, foreign phrases, definitions, etc.
  - Main products of a country or state
  - Climate zones

- Drawings, Illustrations, Photos and Printouts –
  - Landforms

- Ethnic dress/costumes
- Flags and other national symbols
- Artistic masterpieces
- Money/currency
- Photos or drawings of famous sites and people
- Timelines of certain events – wars, battles, women's movements, ruler's lifetime, etc.
- Photos of ethnic meals, from cookbooks or your kitchen
- Drawings or illustrations of inventions, machines, ships, etc.

- Maps –
    - Battles, wars, countries involved in them
    - Countries which share a common language or religion
    - Areas of cultural influence/practice
    - The world at the time of a certain ruler or event
    - Record of an explorer's travels
    - A series of maps showing a country's growth or empire's decline
    - The spread of an epidemic or disease
    - Map showing location of native tribes' homelands
    - Climate zones and growing zones
    - Areas of agricultural production

- Copywork –
    - Quotes from famous or influential people
    - Lyrics to the national anthem
    - Patriotic poetry
    - Foreign language phrases and words, with translations
    - Portions of important civil documents
    - Important speeches
    - Campaign and recruiting slogans
    - State and national motto

Your notebook then should grow and expand as your studies do the same. A six-year old's notebook would look much different, naturally, than a 12 year-old's, but they may contain some of the same information, at appropriate levels of course, and in different ways. Where the six-year old may have a drawing or coloring page of a flag, for example, the 12 year old can give a history of its development, or a copywork of flag etiquette rules, or a biography of its designers. As I said above, notebooks are almost living things, ever-growing, ever-changing records of your learning journey.

Your notebooks should also contain informational reports on the various countries and states that you study. These can take many forms, from posters to fill in the blank printouts to written narrations. You can visit countries again and again, as your student matures, adding more and more information as you wish. Or you can choose an age or a time and delve as deeply into the subject as your child's maturity level will allow. (It is certainly advisable to pay repeated visits to your home country and local area, as that will be of the utmost importance to your child as she grows into adulthood.) Some believe that you should "cycle" through history at least 3 times, 2 times at minimum, so that your student can be assured a thorough understanding of it. I say the same should hold true for all the areas of social studies.   And the second and third time around, you'll have your notebooks there to serve as reminders – instant review, if you will – and a foundation upon which to build your newfound knowledge.

Conclusion

History, geography, culture and citizenship shape our pasts and our futures. They don't have to be daunting or intimidating subjects to approach, however, and they don't have to be costly in either time or money. In fact, social studies may be the easiest of all the academic subjects to teach on the cheap, because so much of the information is right there in front of us, in our daily lives. The tools necessary for teaching social studies are few, can be very inexpensive and can last for years, so that whatever initial investment we may have to make is returned year after year as we continue on our way without further purchases. Homeschooling social studies on the cheap is both rewarding and exciting, and well worth giving a try!

∞∞∞

Science and Nature

Introduction

Science, like maths, often causes a great deal of fear and anxiety among homeschoolers trying to teach on the cheap. And yet, when you stop and consider that science is really only the study of the natural world and how it is ordered, you have to wonder why the fuss? There's a great big world out there to wonder at, to ask questions about, and to find out how it all goes together – your classroom is as close as your doorstep, your fingertips, or your kitchen.

Also, much like maths, there are certain topics and concepts that should be covered by the time a student is ready for high school. However, what is studied when is only determined by the student's age and ability levels and interests. I recommend cycling through each topic at least twice in the elementary years, to ensure that they are learned and understood fully. A 6 year old can learn the names of the different types of clouds, for example, or give a good example of how friction works, but isn't quite ready yet to study weather forecasting in any type of detail, or just how friction affects a runaway object. Since the list of science topics is much longer than the list of maths concepts, I've included it in the Appendix, rather than here in the chapter. Also, you won't find any science listed in the scope and sequence in the Appendix, as I've reserved you the right to choose what to teach exactly when. At the end of this chapter is my list of science/nature related things a child should *do* before reaching his middle teens, however, as it is short enough to be included here in the text and not relegated to the Appendix. I've also included a list of the scientists, inventors and innovators that children often find the most fascinating. I'm sure you'll think of many more to add.

The sciences can be studied using living books – literature – but they are best studied as da Vinci, Pasteur, even Edison studied – through doing. Oh, some texts are necessary, to fill in the background information, teach the terminology, and to impart all those "laws" that govern this big world of ours. Others, particularly fiction titles and biographies, come in handy for the showing the science in motion. Biographies of famous scientists show the science in discovery – you can follow along as the scientist or inventor makes their great discoveries or creations. But if you want your children to really become excited about science, to really gain a love of learning about the way the world works, they must *DO* as well as read. A good balance of texts and hands-on opportunities makes for the best science programs.

Recommended Resources for Science Study

There are a few resources I couldn't put my science program together without, and wouldn't want you to do without either. We have a top-notch science encyclopedia, from Usborne Books. (The Kingfisher edition is very nice, too.) A good animal encyclopedia is good to have on hand, too, for those times when you just have to know the difference between Asian and African elephants, for example. We have made use of several of Janice van Cleave's *…..for Every Kid* series. These are nice because they give the information in small bites, followed by hands-on activities that show that principle in action. The DK *Eyewitness* series has some very nice science-related titles, packed with photos, illustrations, charts and whatnot, with small bits of text interspersed. (These are perfect for the visual learner, as each is a feast for the eyes.) Perfect for the beginning reader is the *Let's Read and Find Out* series. Their information and easy-to-read texts are at just the right level for the younger student. Some tools or equipment I wouldn't do without are our microscope, magnifying glasses, "bug" jar, underwater viewers, (both homemade) and our telescope. Now, some of these were large investments, but buying a good quality telescope, for example, is an investment that should last a lifetime. And, of course, I didn't buy all that all at once. (You should know me by now – I do without, spreading purchases out over time. I've taken advantage of several really nice bargains, too, to acquire our science stuff.)

Studying the Natural Sciences

The Three Types of Natural Sciences

There are three types of the so-called "natural" sciences:

1. Life sciences – biology, botany, zoology, anatomy, etc.
2. Earth sciences – geology, geophysics, oceanography, meteorology, climatology, etc.

3. Physical sciences – physics, chemistry, astronomy, etc.

These are the branches or categories of science that most concern school children. A firm basis in the natural sciences will give them the knowledge they need to understand the world around them and how it works. Other types of "formal" sciences include computer science, engineering, architecture, cybernetics and kinetics. These don't tell us so much about how the world works, but how man-made creations function, or how man functions within his man-made world. (A solid foundation in the natural sciences will prepare a student interested in a career in one the formal sciences, so their importance to a child's education is essential, regardless of their future plans.)

Some homeschoolers "cycle" through these 3 natural sciences every four years, choosing to break the physical sciences into chemistry and physics, creating a four year rotation of earth science and astronomy, biology, chemistry and physics. Others prefer to cover all three (or four, however you may view it) every year. Still others tend to "take it as it comes" – either using their literature selections as a "jumping off point" for their science studies, or choosing to use delight-directed studies and simply going with their child's interests. Some use a different approach to science every year. I don't suppose it really matters, as long as the basics are covered by the time the child is ready for high school/upper level science learning.

Unit Studies vs. Literature-based Studies vs. Purchased Curriculum

Let's look at some pros and cons of the three most popular approaches homeschoolers take to teaching science.

- Unit Studies
    - Pros –
        - can be individualized to suit your needs, schedule, or child's interests
        - can be created using materials, texts, etc. that you have at hand, making them rather inexpensive to do

- can be used with more than one age group/ability level
    - Cons –
        - can produce a choppy or slapdash program, with little carry-over of knowledge or skills
        - can be time-intensive to create on your own
        - can be expensive to purchase pre-made

- Literature-based Studies
    - Pros –
        - Can be based on literature you have, making them inexpensive to do
        - Can be used with more than one age group/ability level
        - Can be customized to suit your needs, interests, or schedule
    - Cons –
        - Can offer little in the way of scientific "meat" and often have to be supplemented with additional texts
        - Can be time intensive to create and plan
        - Few opportunities for purchasing strictly science units (many literature based unit studies include science, but you also get history, language, geography, etc.)
        - Can produce random science opportunities

- Purchased Curriculum
    - Pros –
        - Offer a set spiral or cycle of skills and sciences
        - Can be purchased to age and ability levels (sort of)
        - Takes responsibility for planning from parent

    - Cons –
        - Often expensive
        - Often require science materials or equipment not readily or easily available in the home

- Often require additional resources or reference texts not easily or inexpensively found
- Often lack in opportunities for hands-on learning

I'll be honest with you, we've never ever purchased a science curriculum that worked for us. It was too slow or too advanced, too hands-on or not enough, too workbookish-texbookish or lacked in opportunities to create a written record. We've tried two Charlotte-Masonish programs that created a notebook as you went along. The one's text was too advanced for my son, while the other's idea of "hands-on" activities was a lot of paper-crafty type things. We've tried activity-based programs that had us scrambling to create a written record of some kind to show that we had, in fact, studied science that year. We've tried work text programs that left us feeling as though we had been traveling in the desert – they were that dry and dull. In short, most science curriculum has let us down.

I don't particularly like the haphazardness of relying on our literature readings to create our science lessons, either. This month it's the *Secret Garden* and botany, while next month it's on to something else. It's a bit too random and hit-and-miss for my tastes. I like to use some literature in our studies, particularly if a book lends itself to enhancing the study, such as *My Side of the Mountain* for biology. I guess you could say I prefer to choose the literature based on the science study, not the other way round.

Unit studies can be a bit slapdash, too, without careful planning. You can create a unit to last a term or even an entire year with some success, and I have and continue to do so. Short term units, though, unless they follow your chosen topic or schedule, often result in much the same as basing your science on your literature selections – more accidental than purposeful.

Now, there are some literature-based unit study curriculum programs out there that do a fairly good job of presenting the science through the literature, and I've based our own science studies on the way they are put together. I first choose the science(s) we'll be focusing on for the term or year. Then, I search for literature that will support the science. Lastly, I find or create enough hands-on experiences to put the "doing" portion of our science learning into action. So, I guess you could say I've harnessed the best of all three. I've eliminated the randomness of the literature-based approach, while still adding a literary element to our studies. I've provided hands-on learning opportunities while keeping the materials I have, or can easily acquire. And through the use of notebooking and lap booking, I've solved the problem of having something to show for all our efforts. Best of all, I can tailor our studies to our needs, interests and abilities.

Sometimes I start with the science, sometimes with the book, and sometimes with the interests of my children. Regardless, once I've found the perfect text, whether non-fiction or fiction title, I see how I can best utilize its information and combine it with hands on activities. That might mean bringing in other resource books to complement or enhance the information it has to offer. Or that could mean that I'll need to find a "follow up" text that completes the term I've chosen for the study. Sometimes, you'll want to take a full year, as I did with the study below. Other times, you might only want to spend a half year, as with our physical science study (we spent the other half of the year studying chemistry.) Or, you can use a lot of little units, only a few weeks or even just a week long, that focus on your chosen topic. (This is particularly easy to do with younger children and things like animal studies, plants, and the weather, as there are many, many books written for that age group on those topics.) Lastly, as we study, we decide how we want to create our science notebooks – these definitions could go in matchbook minit books, while that chart would make a nice notebooking entry. As we've built our history and language notebooks, and as we've constructed our math journals as we've traveled along with our studies, so too do we create our science notebooks, growing and changing them as our studies grow and change.

How All This Works

Here's a sample lesson plan from a human body study we completed last school year:

Human Body

Length of study: 28 weeks
Texts Used: *Blood and Guts*

Galen and the Gateway to Medicine
Janice van Cleave's Food and Nutrition for Every Kid
Usborne's Encyclopedia of Science

Sample week:
1.) Read Heart chapter in Blood and Guts
2.) Look at heart and circulatory system in Encyclopedia
3.) Choose one or two experiments/activities from Blood and Guts
4.) Do experiments/activities and notebook about it
5.) Read next chapter in Galen

(The van Cleave book was used to complete the year – we spent 10 weeks after we finished with *Blood and Guts* learning about nutrition.)

Notebooking and Lap booking for Science

Notebooking and lap booking are excellent ways to record your science learning. So much of science information is in small bits – definitions, terms, formulas, "laws," cycles, etc. that lend themselves well to the small format offered by lap booking's mini-book components. On the other hand, science activities and experiments can be best described in narratives (science narrations, if you will) that can be either written or dictated by the student and placed into a notebook. Charts, illustrations and diagrams – the engaged narrations of science reading and activities - can also become additions to a notebook. We also keep a science log, recording what we read and when, and what we did and when. That aids in seeing just how much science was completed, especially when it feels as though we've not been doing anything much in science, or after returning to lessons from a break for the holidays or illness or Real Life. We can easily see where we to pick up where we left off, what topics may need a brief review, or the fact that we have actually been doing quite a bit of science, but it just doesn't feel like it.

For our science notebooks, I've preferred to combine cardstock pages for attaching the lap booking components, as they can be added to a binder and still leave room for the notebooking pages. Otherwise, you're trying to figure out to fold a large sheet of paper to fit it in the lap book folder, or your lap book folder becomes very bulky from all the "big" pages attached to it. A larger binder than one might think necessary is actually better for this lap-note style of notebook. That provides plenty of room for the slight bulk of the folded mini-book components, without the worry of having to replace a smaller binder part-way through the year.

Nature Study

I would be greatly amiss if I did not include a section on nature study in this book, as it can be an integral part of any science program, or even be the entire basis for an elementary science program. Charlotte Mason advocated the practice of nature study, and many other educators wholeheartedly agree that the concept is an effective and fun way to add science learning to a child's education.

Nature study is simply that – a study of the natural world around you. It can be regimented and scheduled – birds this year, trees next, constellations the year after that. Or more of a "take it as it comes" kind of thing, or a bit of both. *We put up the new bird feeders, so let's learn about birds this winter. We're going to the beach this summer, so let's spend some time studying shells, tides and beach birds and other shoreline creatures.* You can even add nature study into your "real" science studies. *Let's learn some constellations while we study astronomy. How about documenting the phases of the moon, too?* Nature study is one of the easiest and least expensive topics to cover in homeschooling, yet so few families actually utilize it.

Nature study is easy to do because nature is always there. Even if you live in the penthouse apartment of a high rise in the middle of a large city, there's nature around you in the form of parks, flower gardens, even the clouds floating by outside your windows. You can even *grow* nature studies in the form of flowers and house plants and household pets. Anytime you study the growth and development of a living thing in its natural environment you are conducting nature study. (So yes, that new baby in the house makes for a great study of human development!)

Set aside a time on a regular basis for your nature studies. Once a week, once a month, every other Saturday, whatever works best for you, is good enough. Then, arm yourself with a few supplies – zipper baggies for specimen gathering; a notebook or clipboard with paper and colored pencils for making drawings, bark rubbings and other observations; field guides for answering those "What is this?" questions, and appropriate clothing. If you need specialized equipment, like underwater viewers, binoculars or a "bug" house, prepare it and have it ready ahead of time. Then, step out the door and let the nature study begin!

I like to take a somewhat active, yet observant role in our nature studies. I have my notebook, I have my guide books, but I also like to just sit and let the children do the finding on their own. Sometimes I'll point something out to them, like that spider web on the fence, or that butterfly that just fluttered past. Other times, their enthusiasm and excitement is all that is needed. I encourage quiet nature study, too, as in drawing a daisy as carefully as they can, or sitting by the creek side and quietly watching the minnows and crawdads in the shallows' shadows. I've made up nature scavenger hunts for them, too, asking them to find certain items such as nuts, flowers, animal tracks, certain types of leaves, etc. so that we may have a directed discussion after we've come inside.

Those discussions after we've left the nature behind and returned home to our natural environment are where the learning takes place in nature study. We lay out our treasures, examine and share our drawings, and pull out our guidebooks and reference materials for further identification of our specimens. Some of this can be done in the field on an individual basis, but for a really good time, try it in a group with everyone around the table, sharing their finds and wondering at the finds of others.

Long-Term Nature Studies

Sometimes, we do take a regimented approach to our studies, like doing a tree observation, or making a weather record. It gives me someplace to go to when I've lost the inspiration for this month's study, or when the weather has been so rotten that no regular study can be conducted.

Tree observations are the simple observations of a tree over a long period of time. This type of nature study awakens the children to the effects the passage of time has on the natural world. Perhaps if you live in the desert or in an area where the climate is always warm, you can find another long term nature observation project, such as bird or insect migrations, or the cycles of rainy and dry weather. To conduct a long-term observation project, the specimen being studied has to be chosen first. Then, a "base" observation is made by taking or making a photo or drawing, recording simple stats like height, diameter, water level, type of tree/insect, location, etc. and your general impressions of the subject. Then, you visit the same subject in a month. Record any changes that have occurred, both to the subject and to its surroundings. (Try to visit at the same time of day each time, so that your observations have as few variables as possible.) Repeat the process for a year or so, recording changes and new observations each time. This type of long-term study also teaches children that not everything needs to be learned in a day, or a week, or even a term's length. Learning and growing never stop, and long term nature studies show that beautifully.

Some topics for long term studies are:

Trees	Weather
Bodies of water – ponds, rivers, creeks or small streams	Backyard birds
	Indoor plants
Night sky	Pets

Indoor Nature Study

I know the term "indoor" nature study seems a bit of an oxymoron, but there will be times, due to weather, illness or other health issues, time constraints and other Real Life factors when getting out and getting into nature are nearly impossible. There's no need to leave nature study behind, though, just because you're stuck indoors. There are things like pet and plant observations that can be conducted in the warmth and comfort of your home. You could set up a bird feeding station and enjoy your feathered friends through the windows. Then there are the *One Small Square* books. These books give you an intimate look at one small one-foot square of various biomes. You can visit the desert from your sofa, take a trip to the swamp without ever leaving your kitchen, or soar through the night sky while, lying comfortably on the rug. We save our *OSS* books for winter time, as winters here in Appalachia often mean days of snow and treacherous roads, making traveling anywhere nearly impossible. (We have other winter time nature topics that we explore, too, like the birds at our feeders, the various tracks in the snow, and identifying trees without their leaves. Snow makes its own fascinating study, too.) Another resource for nature study is the *Kids' Nature Book*, as it gives ideas for stories, poems, crafts and other "indoor" projects for each of its nature study topics. (It provides a year's worth of ideas for studying the wonderful outside world.)

Nature Study Resources

When it comes to other resources for nature study, I would highly recommend some form of tree, flower, bird and insect identification guide for your local area. Make sure your guides are in full color and provide some sort of brief description of the wildlife, if nothing else. It can be difficult to distinguish one vireo from another, for example, without knowing exactly where its grey streaks and patches are, or just which daisy is which without a description of their sizes. There are inexpensive "pocket" guides, small field guides with plastic covers for protection against the natural elements, and of course the Internet has many sites which can help you identify the stuff your children have brought home. (Unless you're planning to take your iPhone or laptop into the wilds with you, it's probably not the best idea to rely on the Web for *all* your identification needs.) There's the classic, *Handbook of Nature Study*, but I found I still needed my color guides, as it is only in black and white. Its information regarding the various aspects of nature that it covers is second-to-none, but when it comes to identifying the nature we find, its black and white illustrations leave much to be desired.

Teach a Respect for Nature

Whatever your political and religious views on the environment or man's role as stewards of the earth might be, you should teach your children some basic rules and respect for the natural world around them. Instilling in them a respect for nature and giving them a few simple, courteous rules to follow means that others who follow after them will be able to enjoy the same walks, fields, woods, nature, just as you and they have enjoyed it.

Here are our rules for nature walks or visits:

1. Leave it as we found it as much as possible. No litter, no disturbances that can't be undone.
2. No digging, except in the sand or mud at the shoreline, where the water will refill the holes.
3. Only one of any of the same specimen per person. Leave the field of daisies or the patch of violets as pristine and unpicked as possible.
4. No sticks except deadfall.
5. Keep the noise to a minimum. Not only does this allow others who might be sharing our space the peace they deserve, but it also allows us to observe more nature, as the birds and small animals aren't frightened away by our noisiness.

The Really Important Stuff

There are some science experiences that no child should miss. Some are more scientific in nature, while others are more nature study-ish. All are things that no elementary child should be denied the opportunity to do or learn at least once. You may not agree with my list. You may have additions you think are just as important. That's alright – just be sure your children are given ample chances to do them.

Here's my list:

- Watch the tide come in, or go out
- Care for a pet
- Plant a seed, watch it grow and care for the plant
- Catch an insect and observe its movements and anatomy
- Watch the moon's phases for a month
- Learn the names of at least three constellations
- Watch a sunset
- Observe water through all three stages of its matter – melt ice until it boils and then watch the steam rise.
- Collect rocks
- Collect shells
- Collect leaves

- Visit a body of water and wade in the shallows, watching for plants and animals
- Visit the same place in every season
- Go to the zoo or wildlife park
- Visit an aquarium
- Look through a telescope
- Visit a planetarium
- Grow crystals
- Observe and record the weather for a month
- Examine your fingerprints under a magnifying glass
- Learn to use a microscope
- Design a contraption using at least 3 simple machines
- Conduct some simple kitchen science experiments – yeast, soda-vinegar fizz, how soap works, find the taste centers of your tongue, etc.
- Plan a meal or week of meals
- Learn basic first aid
- Learn basic pet first aid for your pet
- Learn and practice basic safety rules – water, road, bicycle, etc.
- Build a working electrical circuit
- Play with magnets
- Learn and practice basic hygiene

Now, as with math, that's not a lot of things to fit into 10 years or so. Most can be accomplished close to home, if not in the home. Most can be fitted into your science studies nicely and neatly, as you come across opportunities in your studies. And all are truly memorable experiences to give to your children.

Putting it All Together

Our nature study isn't as routine or as regular as some. We typically "do" a nature study once a month. Sometimes we'll take a whole day – a Friday when we need a break or a sunny Saturday – and simply indulge ourselves in nature. Other times, we'll take advantage of the season or time such as when the trilliums bloom in the spring, or after a good hard rainfall has filled the stream near our house, to visit a certain spot for a certain reason to make sure our observations are what we want them to be. Then there are those glorious moments when the nature comes to us, as when the bluebirds invaded our backyard and made good use of our feeding station on their northward migration a few years ago.

I do know homeschoolers who schedule their nature study on a regular basis. I tried this and found that Real Life interfered more often than not.

You can't guarantee that it won't rain on Thursday, every Thursday, for an entire year just so you can get your nature walk in. I also found that scheduling our nature study often took the spontaneity out of it. I was trying too hard to find stuff for us to study or observe that I often missed the natural opportunities right in front of me. So, now, I just plan on two nature studies a month. I don't schedule them in on any certain days, though Fridays do seem to have better luck than Thursdays ever were. I simply plan on two nature days a month. And so far, it's working for us. We can take a hike through the local state park, or identify the weeds in the flower garden after we pull them. We can watch the moon travel through the sky or find the North Star through our telescope on a particularly fine evening. If there is something seasonal that needs our attention, we can revel in its beauty when it is at its prime, not when our schedule permits. I guess you could say we've taken a more natural approach to nature study.

Conclusion

Combining nature study with more formal studies of the natural sciences will provide your children with a firm foundation for future scientific learning. Teaching them to respect and enjoy the natural world around them can lead to a lifetime of memorable experiences. Giving them the opportunity to experience science and nature first-hand with you, and by themselves, with guidance and through sheer serendipitous discovery, will add so much more to their education and to their lives than textbook and worksheets ever could. Bring science and nature to life by making it a part of their lives. There's a big wide world out there, for free. Go for it!

∞ ∞ ∞

Art and Music

Introduction

The arts are one area where many homeschoolers, even veteran homeschoolers, seem to neglect every now and then as the pressures and daily grind of the "important stuff" takes its toll on even the best-laid plans for adding some culture into your children's education. And yet, without that art and music, at least, we end up with students who become bored and boorish, dulled with the lack of beauty in their atmosphere and learning.

As the great painter Marc Chagall said, "Art seems to me to be a state of soul more than anything else." By exposing our children to great artworks and musical compositions, we are feeding their souls, their hearts - the very preciousness that dwells within them. We are training their ability to see and know beauty in all its forms. We take them from being mere human beings to being more human. So, put the math aside, let the grammar go for a day, history and geography can wait an hour or two, and that science experiment will still be there tomorrow. Indulge your souls a bit. Experience a taste of sweet creativity.

The arts, of course, encompass much more than art and music, but they are the two most easily dealt with in a home setting. Yes, drama is important, as is dance. Without architecture, the world would fall about our ears (or at least the ceiling would) but those are rather difficult to approach from the comfort and ease of your home classroom. Watching a play live is an experience no child should ever be denied, but in my experience, most theater companies won't fit in my family room, nor do they hold performances while our school is in session every morning. Dance is a little more accessible, through video performances, but again, the best experience is a front row center seat, and they are not easily had on my homeschooling budget. Architecture is, well, so *there*, as in you have to go *there* to see it. You can study the local architecture of the buildings in your town or neighborhood, or peruse books of famous buildings, but to see the really *great* stuff typically requires things like plane tickets and hotel rooms and trips to Paris or London or Rome. Not likely to happen too quickly when you're homeschooling on the cheap, are they?

So, that leaves us with the two most easy to be had and to be had cheaply – art and music. Great artworks can be placed in the hands of our children for the cost of a print, or the printer ink and paper to make a print. The masterpieces of the great composers can be enjoyed as we drive to the market, or as we read or work. No, it's not a symphony hall, but our home entertainment system can enthusiastically pour Mozart out the windows till the neighbors complain. (Not that we've ever done that, mind you……) Most public libraries have oversized artwork books, either of individual artists or collections. Most libraries have some access, either CD's, tapes, or digital files, of many of the music world's greatest composers. The Internet is another source for art and music selections. It's out there, waiting for you, ripe and plump for the picking. All you have to do is set your mind to it and go for it. Feed their hearts and souls, as well as their minds!

Art

Our art program consists of two portions - picture or artist study and drawing instruction. Artist study (also known as picture study) gives us exposure to and experience with the great masterpieces and masters of art. Drawing instruction serves many functions, from training hand and eye, to creative expression, to a solid foundation for further types of artistic pursuit.

Picture or Artist Study

When it comes to our study of art, I've taken another page from Charlotte Mason. In an age when only the children of the richest and most powerful had access to the great masterpieces, she advocated art for all through picture study. She would acquire reproductions for her students to observe, discuss and, if so inclined, reproduce themselves. Charlotte Mason's idea of picture study was a bit too formal for me, though, so we don't get quite as involved with it as she did.

I choose 4 to 6 artists for us to study each year. Sometimes, I'll choose a style or "school" of art, other times a time period, other times a theme, and use that as the basis of choosing our artists. It really depends on what we've done in the past, what artworks I can find to provide for my children to use and what else we may be doing in our studies. For example, Post-Impressionism and Modern art accompanied our study of history from 1850 to the present, while a study of famous female artists followed us through ancient history. A showing at a local gallery led to a side trip through mixed media artists one year. So, you choose who you'd like to focus on depending on your mood, your other educational plans, or a happy circumstance in the local art world.

Next, I choose the pieces we will be studying. Choosing 4 to 6 artists a year allows us to study 6 to 10 pieces by each artist a year. The obvious choices are the artists' most famous, best known works. Then, smaller, lesser known pieces are used, if necessary, to fill in. I choose these based on several things: their similarity (or lack of) with the well-known "masterpieces," their personal appeal (not all art is for all age groups, or all households,) and their availability (if you can't print it, buy it, or at least view it on the computer monitor, it's not much use, is it?) The next step is to obtain, through printing or purchasing, the chosen artworks. I typically print ours off from one of several online art galleries, but I have been known to purchase the postcard-sized masterpieces from Dover Publishing. (They have some wonderful collections of full-color artworks, nicely formatted into postcard size.) After that, it's simply waiting for the day and time and study art!

Here's how we conduct our picture/artist studies:

1. Show the children the artwork. (If possible, have enough copies so that all children can actually hold one in their hands and not have to share.)
2. Allow them 5 to 10 minutes to study the artwork - looking at it, making observations about it, commenting on it, etc.
3. Lead them to a discussion of the artwork. *Do you like it? What's happening here? Does it remind you of anything or another piece of art you've seen? When do you think it was made? What type of composition is it – landscape, portrait, grouping, still life? etc.*
4. OPTIONAL STEP: If you'd like to delve into the technicalities of art, you can proceed into a lesson or review or discussion of the various technical aspects – line, texture, medium, light source, shadow, color, theme, etc. (We do some of this, but not a lot. We do enough to develop a working vocabulary when discussing artworks, especially when discussing and reading

about the artists. I feel, however, that picking apart every piece of artwork we encounter is like picking apart every poem you read for rhyme scheme and imagery and whatnot. After a while, you lose the beauty of the thing for all the tedious analysis.)

5. Learn a bit about the artist – name, time in which he lived, country of birth or of residence when he painted the particular piece, what era of art he belonged to – Impressionist, Renaissance, Pop Art, etc. – who some of his contemporaries were, major societal or cultural events during his lifetime, etc. Many artists are feature in biographies for children. There's a wonderful series, *Getting to Know the World's Greatest Artists* by Mike Venezia, that are just complete enough to satisfy, without being so in-depth as to stupefy your students. Knowing the man or woman behind the artwork and the times in which he or she lived and worked and created can often lead to a greater understanding and appreciation for the art itself. (If you'd like, you could create or fill out a simple biography of the artist for your notebooks.)

6. After you've studied both the artist and the artwork, it's time to get your creativity flowing and produce or reproduce some great art of your own. A simple reproduction of the piece might suffice, especially if you have less-than-enthusiastic artists-to-be in your crew. If you'd like to try your hand at something a little different, or need some great ideas to boost your hands-on art experiences, I'd highly recommend *Discovering Great Artists* and *Masterpiece of the Month*. The first is a wonderful resource full of projects and ideas for many of the world's most famous artists. Lie on your back and paint or draw on paper stuck to the underside of the table while learning about Michelangelo's Sistine chapel, or create your own El Greco using a face or head shot from a magazine. The second, geared for classroom teachers but easily adapted to homeschooling, gives you a famous piece of art, and then a project based upon it. Some artists are represented more than once, and it is a much smaller volume than *DGA*, but we've had some enjoyable experiences using it.

7. Repeat next week with a new piece of art. If you use up all the ideas in your resource books before you've finished with the artist in question, don't forget to simply have the child try their hand at reproducing the artwork. We typically do one to two hands-on projects per artist, rather than one every week, but every now and then we still do a reproduction activity. It's good training for the eye and the attention to detail.

For older students try allowing them choose one of the artworks for further study. They can do a more in-depth biography of the artist, or delve deeper into the time period. Locate where the masterpiece is currently residing and any restoration or research that art historians or curators have conducted on it. Did the artist do any preliminary sketches or rough drafts before completing the final piece, and if so, are they available for public viewing anywhere? This type of "getting into the art" is not only a good exercise for academic reasons, but it also allows them to grow closer to the artwork and the artist. My daughter, at age 9, fell head over heels for Vincent Van Gogh. She still carries a color print from that study three years ago in her main subjects binder. It's his *The Bedroom*, from his time at the Yellow House in Arles. She finds it appealing, but can't really say why. (I have a feeling it has something to do with the intimacy of it all – a glimpse into the personal life of this otherwise almost unapproachable, tragic master.)

Why Drawing Instruction?

Teaching children to draw, and drawing with them, is an invaluable skill. Almost as important as teaching them to write, teaching them to draw gives them a creative outlet that can be practiced almost anywhere, with anything. The first recorded expressions of human existence, the cave paintings, are perfect examples of this – created with whatever was on hand, depicting everyday scenes and ordinary sights. Drawing *with* them typically shows them that they need never fear for their own abilities. (Unless you are a famous-artist-turned-homeschooler, your abilities probably aren't much better than theirs. It evens the playing field a bit.) It also serves to show them that art, however solitary a pursuit it might seem can actually be quite sociable.

Drawing requires hand-eye coordination, attention to detail, and fine motor skill development. All are important skills for academic success, as well as success in Life in general. (Now if that's not enough of an incentive to begin drawing instruction with your children, what more do you need?) Children who draw early and often find themselves developing handwriting skills faster and easier. They find they can attend to readings and studies for longer and longer periods of time. And they find sports skills, crafts and other art endeavors, and even body awareness all improved through the practice of drawing. Why?

Because drawing engages both the physical and the mental realms and it engages both sides of the brain at once. You are physically moving your hand and eyes together, seeing the shapes, tracing the lines, reproducing the image before you, whether real or imaginary, through physical labor. At the same time, your mind is processing light and shadow, shape and form, detail and background. Your brain is fully engaged in the process of creating, as if the chair or the flowers or the person weren't really there, except in your mind and on your paper. That type of mental focus doesn't come often, especially in children. They flit from one activity to another, from one whim or fancy to the next. This week it's fish fingers, next it's pizza. Today, everything has to be orange or yellow or green. Tomorrow it can't be anything but purple or blue or red. And many times, our own educational systems and routines foster this. Yes, there is merit in learning in 10 to 15 minute blocks. But drawing gives us the opportunity to stop time, or at least slow it down, as we take our time and focus, really focus, on the task and the model at hand.

Drawing serves as the foundation for nearly every other visual art. Sculptors draw and sketch before they place hand to clay or chisel to marble. Painters draw and sketch long before they pick up their brushes and palettes. Every great piece of architecture began on a piece of paper shortly after it was dreamed up in the architect's head. Even fabric artists and fashion designers typically begin with rough sketches of the desired finished items. So, no matter where your child's artists travels may lead, it's a good bet that drawing will help them along the way.

Drawing is also one of the least-expensive forms of art you can engage in. A sketchbook, a few good old fashioned #2 pencils (to start - add better drawing pencils later,) a sturdy eraser, and maybe a few good quality colored pencils are all you need. My children insist that a pencil box or pouch is also necessary, to keep everything handy and neat. His is blue, hers pink, mine green. No trip to the art store necessary, no great big investment needed. The hardest thing about buying drawing supplies is choosing your color of pencil box, apparently.

How We Learn to Draw

I begin drawing instruction with my children when they are very young, 4 to 5 years old, using the *DrawWriteNow* books. These wonderful books have simple drawings, broken down into easy-to-follow and reproduce steps, accompanied by 4 sentences or lines for copywork practice. The books are categorized by topics – Animals, Farm, etc. so that it is fairly easy to match up this week's picture with a story, unit study, season or holiday, or interest. You can try other books if you prefer, or none at all, but DWN has never left me down.

We progress from DWN to Mark Kistler's books. He teaches some serious art skills and concepts through his silly cartooning lessons. Children learn perspective, shading, texture and a whole host of other topics while drawing space aliens wearing funny hats and living in architecturally impossible high rises. The fun factor alone should be enough to convince you to try Capt. Mark's series of books!

After that, we get serious about art, turning to Betty Edward's *Drawing on the Right Side of the Brain* and the accompanying workbook. By the time a child is 12 or 14 and has had some basic drawing instruction, she is ready to tackle Betty's program. Betty teaches artistic *seeing* as much as she does drawing, and the development from child artist to accomplished artist is amazing to watch. Once a teen has finished Betty's book and workbook exercises, if completed with diligence and the regular practice she suggests, he should be ready and able to draw anything he sees or imagines, as realistically or fanciful as his creativity requires.

Once a teen can draw with confidence and competence, if he chooses to continue on with another form of art – painting, sculpting, carving etc. – there are many resources, from adult classes to video courses to simply letting him go and see what he can develop on his own, to develop his skills and interests further. Drawing opens the door to a world of artistic possibilities. And if he chooses to never draw anything ever again (although I've never actually heard of anyone who spent years learning to draw who didn't at least doodle and dabble for his own benefit) he's still learned valuable skills of observation, patience, diligence and attention to detail that are his forever.

The Place of Crafts

We incorporate crafts in our homeschooling, though not on a formal basis. I find most crafts to be too uncreative – there's only one real outcome. I prefer to teach my children *handi*crafts, such as woodworking, embroidery, sewing, weaving, knitting or crocheting. These are useful and creative outlets which produce products that last far longer than construction paper flowers or milk carton houses. I sometimes use crafts as a fun lesson aid, all the more the better if what I'm teaching is an authentic craft from a certain time period or culture. Sometimes a certain craft project can actually be used to enhance a lesson, such as making a "treasure map" or creating paper doll soldiers in proper uniforms. I look for craft projects that can add to our history lessons, and of course we do quite a few holiday related crafts, but I leave the majority of the crafty creations for my children's free time. They are well supplied with glue, glitter, construction paper, tissue paper, pipe cleaners (even the really fuzzy ones,) craft sticks, paper tubes and a whole host of other assorted crafting "essentials." I've even purchased a few crafty idea books to add to our ever growing box of supplies. We seldom have a boring rainy afternoon if the craft box comes out. I just prefer to keep the crafts out of my classroom, for the most part.

Music

Plato is quoted as having said, "Music gives soul to the universe, wings to the mind, flight to the imagination, and charm and gaiety to life and to everything." Our long-ago Greek knew more than he realized, said more than he could ever come to know with that statement. Recent research has shown that exposure to music may help a child's reading ability, IQ level, and the development of certain areas within the brain. Music has been scientifically proven to lower stress and add joy and fun to life. Learning to play an instrument teaches discipline and gives one a sense of achievement. Plato's comments about music hit the note, sharp and true, about 2,500 years ago.

Like art, I use a two-pronged approach to music in my homeschool. We do music appreciation, in the form of composer study, and we make an endeavor to see that each child learns to play at least one instrument. Thus, we cover both sides of music - hearing and doing.

Music Appreciation or Composer Study

Charlotte Mason devotees practice composer study, which is really just a formalized version of music appreciation. Whether you follow a schedule and routine as they do, or simply expose your children to the great composers through lots of opportunities to hear their works, you'll accomplish the same goals – familiarizing your children with great composers and the great music they created.

Our composer study takes much the same form as our artist studies. We listen, we discuss, we learn. Instead of trying to reproduce though, since that is something quite altogether different with music, we "judge" – choosing our favorite piece and telling why we liked it best and what made it different from the other pieces by the same composer. Then, it's time to move on to a new composer and new selections for study. I try to time our composers and our artists, so that we move to a new one of each at the same time. Some artists and composers, however, don't want to cooperate with that plan, hanging on long after they should have retired, because they've sparked a love and a longing for more. I don't mind, really, for that is what art and music appreciation is for – inspiring a love for the beautiful things in life.

I often do attempt to match our artists and composers, and to that end, I've included a list matching some of the more famous artists and composers in the Appendix. It is easier when discussing background material, cultural influences, societal changes, etc. as I can use the same resources, the same references, for both studies. The two often complement each other nicely, showing the "tastes" of the time running through both art forms. Since I often try to match my artist studies with other portions of our learning, as mentioned previously, our composer studies fall in line as well. This gives a nice effect overall – studying a time period AND its culture through its art and music. You're hearing and seeing what the people of the day heard and saw, bringing the past to life in a whole new way.

What we do for composer study isn't that complicated, not nearly as complex as artist study. I'll choose 4 to 6 composers to study for the year. Then, the selections are determined by two factors – those that are best known, and those which I have or can gain access to recordings of. For example, you can't study Tchaikovsky without listening to the *Nutcracker Suite* or the *1812 Overture*, but you could do without *Swan Lake* if your local library doesn't have it and your computer's speakers are shot. There are many "greatest hits" type collections of the more well-known masters available. I've even seen them for as little a dollar or two in discount bins. (If you're not so particular about *who* is playing the music, they can be a good investment. One of the few homeschool related purchases I make every year is to add to our growing collection of music, even if it's only a disc or two. Great music is something that never goes out of fashion, and creating a home library of the masters is something you'll never really regret.)

After I've selected the composers we'll study, we simply choose a CD and play it. We play it in the car, while we're eating, while we're studying, while we're doing our chores, while we're playing games, in short it becomes the soundtrack for our lives for a while. Then, after a week or so of listening, I'll "introduce" the children to the composer. Mike Venezia has also written a series of biographies of the *World's Greatest Composers*, so doing so is quite easy. Again, I'm looking for a spouting of facts, dates, etc. I'm not even that concerned if they remember that Mozart is considered a "Classical" composer, while Chopin was a "Romantic." I'm more concerned with them remembering that Mozart lived well before Chopin, or that one was German and the other Polish and French, and that they wrote vastly different styles of music.

Once we've established who it is we're listening to, I allow the children to each pick a "target" piece – by choice of favorite. (They've been listening to the works for at least a week to two weeks, so they've had plenty of time to form opinions and know what appeals to them best. If they are stubborn or reluctant to choose, I will either, if possible, allow them to listen to more of the composer's works, or "volunteer" a favorite for them) This gives them something to sink their ears into, to mix a metaphor. This one piece is theirs to study, to internalize, for the next few weeks. When we are finished with that composer, it will be their job to present their piece, a short explanation of why it appealed to them, and any other information they can research on the piece. This combines the feeding of the soul and the mind, keeping both growing. Now, as I mentioned, sometimes we get "stuck" on a composer. When this happens, it's a good thing really, because it means that they've found his or her works so enjoyable that they want to delve deeper, hearing more of the music. Unlike junk food, where you can have too much of a good thing, more Beethoven is not.

If possible, you should try and include a live performance at some point. Even if it's just the local high school orchestra, hearing the music live gives it a whole new dimension, just as seeing the real artwork in a museum adds a scope and depth to it that you just can't experience at home with a print. Something to keep in mind – oftentimes, music students at college or university are required to give solo performances. These are often free to the public, but go largely unadvertised. If you are near enough to a campus with a music program, contact them for a list of dates of these free opportunities and try to work one in, even if it means a road trip.

One last note of advice – don't restrict yourself to the great "masters" only. There are many "modern" composers of "popular" music who have had great influence on music, society and culture. Don't forget the likes of the Dorsey Brothers, Glenn Miller, Lennon and McCartney, Dylan, Kristofferson, Cash, or Guthrie. Their contributions to music are still being felt and heard on the airwaves today. Just as you shouldn't neglect folk music in your history and cultural lessons, don't neglect the men and women who have helped shaped the music of the modern world. Who knows? They may be considered the "masters" of tomorrow.

Learning to Play

As we've already discussed, learning to play an instrument goes much further than simply developing a student's art or cultural literacy. I've been a musician for most of my life, learning to play my first instrument at age 8 and going on to be a French horn major at university. I can personally attest to the benefits of learning to play – I'm still learning and practicing to this day. You needn't have my experience with music, though, to teach your children. In fact, I would encourage you to learn alongside them, if you've never played anything more than the radio. The joy and benefits aren't just for the young!

I like to start my children where I started, with the recorder. It's an ancient instrument, with sheet music still around from the Middle Ages. It's also very easy to learn to play, and very inexpensive to purchase. There are many good models available for $5 to $10. I would stay away from the cheaper plastic ones, especially those found in toy departments and discount stores, as they are often not properly tuned, toned or of good quality materials. There's nothing more frustrating than trying to learn to play a squeaking cheapie that is ever in danger of breaking. Spend a few dollars more for an instrument worth having. Then, spend a few dollars more on a book to teach not only how to play the recorder (some come with these, and they are little more than fingering charts and a few tips for players) but that also teaches music theory. That's the nitty-gritty of how to read music – note names, time signatures, key signatures, sharps, flats, rests, etc. What is learned on soprano recorder is the same for any treble clef instrument, from piano to violin, guitar to French horn. I use Penny Gardner's *Nine-Note* method with my children, partly because it is a good, solid foundation in recorder player and music theory, and partly because Mrs. Gardner has arranged a whole host of tunes in duets and trios. This offers homeschool students the opportunity to play in a group, hearing harmonies and countermelodies, something that most programs do not. She has also arranged several hymn books and Christmas book, as well, offering opportunities for possible performances, even if they're only for family and friends.

Another good place to start is with guitar. Again, the learning is transferrable to other instruments later. The investment in a student or child-sized guitar is considerably more than that of a recorder, but well worth it if your child enjoys playing. The folks at the Alfred music company have been publishing "how to play" books for almost 100 years, and their beginner guitar books are quite possibly the best around, as they teach chords, strumming, note "picking" and music theory all at the same time. They even have DVD lessons available now, for the visual learner.

I'm often asked about piano for young children. I find that piano is a very hard place to start, for the child and the family. First, there's the cost involved, unless you already own one. Then, there are maintenance costs of keeping it tuned. Even electronic keyboards can be expensive, though cheaper than their acoustic counterparts. Also, many children simply can't learn to play the piano without a tutor. This adds to the expense, as well. Lastly, from the child's point of view, until his hands are large enough to span the keys properly, his fine motor skills developed enough to handle the speed and dexterity the piano requires, and his legs long enough to reach the pedals, he's going to find his piano practicing and playing frustrating and anything but fun and stress free. His experiences will be anything but the idyllic scene that introduces this chapter. I prefer to wait until the child has reached age 10 or even older, to begin piano. Again, Alfred's has published a wonderful series of beginner books for the older student, and being more physically prepared to tackle the instrument seems to make learning to play easier, faster and definitely more enjoyable.

Of course, regardless of the instrument, the child has to practice it, and regularly, for any real success to be gained, or any level of competence attained. I hold mine to at least 20 minutes a day, 5 days a week. (When first starting out, only require 10 minutes a day, please.) You'd be amazed at how far they can come in such a short time, if that short time is observed daily. Keeping practice time short avoids boredom, overtiring of developing muscles, and yet still affords enough practice to steadily develop those muscles and playing ability. As the child becomes more competent, she will often practice well beyond her set daily limit, as the joy of playing and the excitement and pride of accomplishment take over.

Please, never, ever use music practice as some form of punishment. If your child sees his instrument as a tool for discipline instead of as a welcoming diversion, his enthusiasm will wane and his playing and learning will suffer. Discipline should be applied to the practice, surely. He can't run off and play baseball if he hasn't put in his practice time. But practice should not be seen as a punishment because he didn't keep his room clean or because he had a fight with his sister, just because he doesn't always enjoy doing it.

Your children may never become virtuosos, or even acquire enough skill to perform before others, but there is too much to be gained from learning to play an instrument to allow it to slip past without trying. And all the whining about practicing and all the funny noises emitting from behind the closed door will eventually pay off, if not in musical ability certainly in many other facets of life and learning. The diligence it takes to really practice an instrument, the pride from knowing you've performed at your best, and the joy of having conquered the "impossible" piece, be it *Hot Cross Buns* or a Beethoven symphony, are things that can never be taken away, things that last you a lifetime.

Conclusion

Giving your children a foundation in the arts doesn't require a great deal of time or money on your part. It doesn't have to be some big, formal thing that you sweat over, but it's far too important to their overall development to miss out on. We take one day a week, typically Friday, and have our art and music "lessons." The musical selections become a part of our daily life, while great artworks can be found in our notebooks, on the front of the refrigerator, and hanging on the walls of our home. We surround ourselves with the beautiful creations of others, and we become inspired to make our own beautiful creations. The state of our souls is apparent in our art and music. Share your souls and your beauty with your world. You, and it, will be better for having done so.

∞ ∞ ∞

Appendix

Scope and Sequence

4 to 8 years old

Language Arts
- Phonics/reading instruction
- Easily reads words at current level of phonics instruction
- Giving adequate engaged or oral narrations of readings up to 10 to 15 minutes in length
- Begin handwriting instruction – one font/style, lower and upper case
- Writing own name
- Copying 2 to 4 sentences/lines
- Composing - either orally or through dictation - short stories, fairy tales, poems, and fables
- Identifies initial capitals and ending punctuations in sentences
- Identifies and constructs complete sentences
- Plays word games
- Reads or is read to for a total of at least an hour a day
- Reads or is read to from a variety of genres – fairy tales, fiction, historical fiction, fables, non-fiction – at age appropriate levels
- Studies at least 3 poets every year
- Memorizes at least 6 poems, songs or Scripture passages per year

Math

Gaining Mastery
- Reading and writing numbers through 1,000
- Counting by 2's, 5's and 10's
- Using ordinal numbers
- Using < and > symbols
- Addition and subtraction facts through 9 + 9 and 18 – 9
- Estimating answers to addition and subtraction problems
- Adding 3 and 4 digit columns of numbers
- Identifies congruent shapes
- Recognizes square, rectangle, circle and triangle
- Compares lengths, areas, and weights
- Measures with non-standard units
- Tells time to the nearest quarter hour

- Makes change with coins and bills
- Knows days of the week and months of the year
- Uses calendar to find dates
- Makes and interprets simple pictographs and bar graphs
- Works with patterns of numbers, shapes, colors, etc. with confidence and ability
    - Adds to existing patterns
    - Completes missing sections
    - Creates new patterns

Actively Learning
- Problem solving strategies
    - Draws diagrams to solve problems
    - Rewords problems
    - Guesses with reasoning
- Estimation skills
- Reading and writing numbers up to 10,000
- Counting by 3's and 4's
- Identifying odd and even numbers
- Identifying fractions as parts of a whole
    - 1/2
    - 1/3
    - 1/4
- Addition and subtraction of 2 digit numbers with and without regrouping (borrowing and carrying over)
- Recognizing lines of symmetry
- Estimating measurements
- Conducting simple probability activities

New Math Introductions
- Uses of a calculator
- Multiplication
- Division

Social Studies
- Family history
- Local history
- Local geography
- Introductory national history
- National and local symbols

- National and local significant figures – heroes, founders, explorers, etc.
- Introductory government/civics
- Introductory economics
- Personal/home address and phone number
- Personal/street/water safety
- Begins to use maps, globes and/or atlases to locate places

Arts
- Identifies differences and similarities in different works
- Identifies colors, light/shadows, themes, medium, etc. in artwork
- Identifies types of instruments – brass, woodwind, string, rhythm – when heard in compositions
- Can express likes and dislikes in art and music pieces
- Studies 4 to 6 artists and composers and their works per year
- Can identify at least one piece by each artist and composer studied
- Knows difference between painting, drawing/sketching, sculpting, collage, watercolors
- Has regular hands-on opportunities to produce or reproduce artwork
- Works with different materials and mediums to produce artwork
- Begins drawing instruction
- Sings and learns 4 to 6 new songs per year
- Begins instrument instruction

Ages 6 to 10

Language Arts

- Completes phonics/reading instruction
- Reads independently for information and enjoyment
- Giving adequate engaged or oral narrations of readings up to 10 to 15 minutes in length
- Continuing handwriting instruction – adds another style – cursive or italics, lower and upper case
- Writing own work in cursive/italics
- Copying 3 to 5 sentences/lines
- Composing short stories, fairy tales, poems, fables, research reports, speeches, descriptive passages, dialogues, and personal letters
- Writes with style, flow and personal voice
- Identifies narrator's point of view and can write in all three points of view
- Identifies initials, abbreviations, personal titles and what they stand for
- Identifies and constructs complete paragraphs
- Identifies and knows how to use nouns, verbs, adjectives and adverbs
- Plays word games
- Reads or is read to for a total of at least two hours a day
- Begins to keep vocabulary lists
- Begins spelling instruction
- Reads or is read to from a variety of genres – fairy tales, fiction, historical fiction, fables, non-fiction – at age appropriate levels
- Studies at least 3 poets every year
- Memorizes at least 6 poems, songs or Scripture passages per year

Math

Gaining Mastery

- Creating, analyzing and solving word problems for all maths concepts
- Estimating numbers with all problems
- Reading and writing numbers to 10,000
- Using standard and non-standard units to measure length, area, volume, weight and temperature
- Telling time to the minute
- Calculating time elapsed
- Finding fractions of whole numbers

- Making, reading and interpreting graphs
- Recognizing 2 dimensional shapes – square, triangle, rectangle, octagon, hexagon, rhombus

Actively Learning
- Using a variety of problem solving strategies to solve multi-step problems
- Rounding skills
- Reading and writing numbers beyond 10,000
- Basic operations through 4 digits
- Symmetry
- Reading and drawing simple coordinate maps
- Terminology and uses of coordinate grids
- Identifying parallel and perpendicular lines
- Comparing fractions
- Making simple scale drawings
- Using sampling techniques to collect data
- Performing simple probability exercises

New Math Introductions
- Using of a calculator in problem solving
- Developing formal math vocabulary – the language of math
- Equivalent fractions
- Adding and subtracting simple decimals
- Using shapes to find patterns
- Right angles
- How different shapes fill a flat surface (tiling)
- Terminology and uses of geometric grid
- Uses and meanings of statistics
- Learning about percents
  - 10%
  - 50%
  - 100%
- Special numbers
  - Factors
  - Multiples
  - Squares

Social Studies
- Introductory world history
- State/Provincial/Regional history
- Intermediate national history
- Introductory national geography
- Introductory world geography
- Intermediate government/civics
- National and world leaders – heroes, founders, explorers, etc.
- Intermediate economics
- Continues to use maps, globes and/or atlases to locate places

Arts
- Identifies differences and similarities in different works
- Identifies colors, light/shadows, themes, medium, etc. in artwork
- Identifies types of instruments by their proper section in the orchestra
- Can express likes and dislikes in art and music pieces
- Studies 4 to 6 artists and composers and their works per year
- Can identify at least one piece by each artist and composer studied
- Has regular hands-on opportunities to produce or reproduce artwork
- Works with different materials and mediums to produce artwork
- Continues drawing instruction
- Sings and learns 4 to 6 new songs per year
- Continues instrument instruction

Ages 10 to 14

Language Arts

- Reads independently for information and enjoyment
- Giving adequate engaged, oral, and written narrations of readings up to 30 minutes in length
- Completes handwriting instruction
- Writing own work in cursive/italics
- Copying 4 to 8 sentences/lines/paragraphs
- Composing short stories, fairy tales, poems, fables, research reports, speeches, descriptive passages, dialogues, essays, personal and business letters
- Writes with style, flow and personal voice
- Identifies narrator's point of view and can write in all three points of view
- Constructs complete essays and other compositions with ease
- Identifies and knows how to use all the parts of speech
- Plays word games
- Reads or is read to for a total of at least two hours a day
- Continues to keep vocabulary lists
- Continues spelling instruction
- Reads or is read to from a variety of genres – fairy tales, fiction, historical fiction, fables, non-fiction – at age appropriate levels
- Studies at least 3 poets every year
- Memorizes at least 6 poems, songs or Scripture passages per year

Math

Gaining Mastery

- Formal mathematical vocabulary
- Estimating and rounding numbers with all problems
- Using calculators in problem solving
- Adding, subtracting, multiplying and dividing with fractions
- Adding, subtracting, multiplying and dividing with decimal numbers
- Computing decimals
- Relating decimals to fractions and percents
- Parallel and perpendicular lines
- Measuring and drawing angles
- Congruent shapes
- Shapes that are the same or similar but different sizes

- Symmetry, reflections and tessellations
- Making equal line segments and perpendicular intersections
- Coordinate graphing
- Drawing and reading maps
- Making scale and perspective drawings
- Collecting and organizing data
- Statistics
    - Mean
    - Median
    - Mode
- Creating and reading graphs
    - Bar
    - Line
    - Picture
    - Circle/pie chart
    - Line
- Measuring
    - Length
    - Area
    - Volume
    - Mass
    - Temperature in both Fahrenheit and Celsius
    - Time
- Circles
    - Diameter
    - Radius
    - Circumference

Actively Learning

- Special numbers
    - Prime
    - Composite
    - Squares
    - Common divisors
    - Cubes
    - Common multiples
- Fraction relationships
    - Comparing
    - Equivalent

- o Improper fractions
- o Reducing fractions
- o Mixed numbers
- o Reciprocals
* Ratio and proportion
* Scientific notation
* Finding greatest common factors and least common multiples
* Using correct formulas to calculate are of a:
  - o Circle
  - o Triangle
  - o Rectangle

New Math Introductions
* Operations with positive and negative numbers
* Square roots

Social Studies
* Intermediate world history
* Advanced national history
* Advanced national geography
* Intermediate world geography
* Advanced government/civics
* National and world leaders – heroes, founders, explorers, etc.
* Advanced economics
* Continues to use maps, globes and/or atlases to locate places

Arts
* Identifies differences and similarities in different works
* Identifies colors, light/shadows, themes, medium, etc. in artwork
* Identifies types of instruments by their proper section in the orchestra
* Can express likes and dislikes in art and music pieces
* Studies 4 to 6 artists and composers and their works per year
* Can identify at least one piece by each artist and composer studied
* Has regular hands-on opportunities to produce or reproduce artwork
* Works with different materials and mediums to produce artwork
* Completes drawing instruction
* Sings and learns 4 to 6 new songs per year
* Continues instrument instruction or begins second instrument

Alphabet Ideas

A – acorn, alligator, alphabet, ambulance, angel, animal, ape, apple, April, astronaut
B - ballerina, balloon, baseball players, bear, bicycle, bird, book, butterfly
C - caboose, cap, castle, caterpillar, clock, clown, cow, crocodile
D - dancer, dinosaur, dog, dolphin, duck
E - ear, Easter, egg, elephant, elves, emperor, emu, engine
F - fairy, farm, fire truck, fish, flag, frog
G - garden, goat, goodnight, goose, gorilla, grandfather/grandmother
H - hat, hedgehog, home, honey
I - ice cream, icicle, igloo, inchworm, inspector, island
J - jam, jeep, jelly, jump, jungle
K - kangaroo, king, kite, kitten, koala
L - ladybug, lamb, leaves, library, lighthouse, love
M - mitten, monkey, moon, mouse, music
N - necklace, neighborhood, nest, night, nurse
O – ocean, octopus, ostrich, olive, ox
P - parade, people, picnic, pony, pumpkin, puppy
Q - queen, quiet, quilt
R - rabbit, rain, rainbow, ribbon, robot, rodeo
S – seashore, snow, space, star, sunshine
T - teddy bear, tiger, toy, train, tree, truck
U - umbrella, uncle, unicorn, United States
V - valentine, vase, vegetable, violin, volcano
W - wagon, wall, water, wind, wings, winter, wish
X – boxcar, exercise, exit, explorer, fox, ox, taxi, x-ray
Y - yak, year, yellow, yo-yo
Z - zebra, zoo, zoom

Phonics Blends

Beginnings
BL
BR
CH
CL
CR
DR
FL
FR
GL
GR
PH
PL
PR
SH
SL
ST
TH
TR
VR
WH
WR

Endings
CH
CK
GH
GHT
LF
LP
LT
MB
ST
TH
TCH
XT

Vowel Blends

AE	EA	IE
AI	EAU	IL
AL	EE	IR
AR	EL	
AU	EI	
AW	ER	
AY	EW	
	EY	
OA	UE	
OE	UI	
OI	UL	
OL	UR	
OO		
OR		
OU		
OW		

Word Families

A	E	I	O	U
ACK	EAR	ICE	OAT	UCK
AD	EAT	ICK	OCK	UG
AIL	EEL	IDE	OG	UMP
AIN	EEN	IFE	OIL	UN
AKE	EEP	IGH	OKE	UNK
ALE	EET	IGHT	OLD	UNT
ALF	ELF	ILE	OLT	
ALL	ELK	ILD	OO	
ALK	ELL	ILK	OOD	
ALM	ELM	ILL	OOF	
AM	ELP	IN	OOK	
AME	EN	INE	OOM	
AN	ENT	ING	OOL	
ANE	EST	IP	OOM	
ANK	ERT	IT	OOP	
ANT			OOT	
AP			OP	
APE			OR	
AR			ORN	
ARE			OT	
ARK			OUGHT	
ART			OULD	
ASH			OUSE	
AT			OUT	
ATE			OW	
AW			OWN	
AY				

Poetry Forms

5 W's Poem   Example:

Line 1: Who   I
Line 2: What   Am writing a poem
Line 3: When   Right now
Line 4: Where   At my desk under the window
Line 5: Why   Because the snowflakes told me to.

◊◊◊◊◊

Diamonte Poetry

Line 1: One word (noun/subject opposite or contrasting to Line 7)
Line 2: Two words (adjectives for line 1)
Line 3: Three words (action verbs that relate somehow to line 1)
Line 4: Four words (first two relate to line 1, last 2 relate to line 7)
Line 5: Three words (action verbs that relate somehow to line 7)
Line 6: Two words (adjectives for line 7)
Line 7: One word (noun/subject opposite or contrasting to line 1)

EXAMPLE:

                         Day
                     Bright, Busy
           Hurrying, Scurrying, Working,
       Happy, Tired, Slower, Restful,
          Reading, Bathing, Sleeping,
               Dark, Peaceful,
                        Night

Cinquains

Line 1: Two syllables OR	Line 1: One word title
Line 2: Four syllables	Line 2: 2 words describing title
Line 3: Six syllables	Line 3: Three word action phrase
Line 4: Eight syllables	Line 4: Four words for emotions
Line 5: Two syllables	related to/about title
	Line 5: One word synonym for title

◊◊◊◊◊

Name Poem

Line 1 - your first name
Line 2 - "It means" then 3 adjectives that describe you
Line 3 - "It is the number" then any number you choose
Line 4 - "It is like" describe a color but don't name it
Line 5 - "It is " and name something you remember experiencing with family or friends that makes you smile to remember
Line 6 - "It is the memory of" and name a person who is or has been important to you
Line 7 - "Who taught me" 2 abstract concepts (such as "honesty")
Line 8 - "When he/she" then refer to something that person did that displayed the qualities in line 7
Line 9 - "My name is" your first name
Line 10 - "It means" and in 1-2 brief sentences state something important you believe about life.

I Am Poem

I am (two special characteristics)

I wonder (something you are actually curious about)

I hear (an imaginary sound)

I see (an imaginary sight)

I want (an actual desire)

I am (the first line of the poem restated)

I pretend (something you pretend to do)

I feel (a feeling about something imaginary)

I touch (an imaginary touch)

I worry (something that really bothers you)

I cry (something that makes you very sad)

I am (the first line of the poem repeated)

I understand (something you know is true)

I say (something you believe in)

I dream (something you actually dream about)

I try (something you make an effort to do)

I hope (something you actually hope for)

I am (the first line of the poem repeated)

Acrostic Poem

Choose a one word title. Write the word vertically on your paper, one letter per line. Each new line of the poem must begin with the letter of the word written on that line.

EXAMPLE:

Spring

S howery mornings
P urple tulips
R ainy afternoons
I ce melting
N ew leaves
G reen everywhere!

◊◊◊◊◊

Clerihews

Rules for writing clerihews:

1. Four lines long.
2. The first and second lines rhyme with each other, and the third and fourth lines rhyme with each other.
3. The first line names a person, and the second line ends with something that rhymes with the name of the person.
4. A clerihew should be funny.

EXAMPLE: My friend Max

Plays a really mean sax.

But he won't play at all

Unless he's facing the wall!

Book Report Ideas

1. Write a newspaper story of the main event of the book.
2. Create a puppet show of the story.
3. Build a diorama of the book's main setting.
4. Write a letter as though you are a character in the book, telling something that happened to you.
5. Make a poster advertising the book, its author or its main character.
6. Create a comic strip of the book's main story.
7. Write a song or poem that tells about the book.
8. Pretend to be a news reporter and give an "on the scene" report from the book's main setting or event.
9. Write and interview of a main character from the book, as though you were writing for a magazine or newspaper.
10. Make a collage of important items in the story.
11. Make a timeline of the story's events.
12. Sculpt or sketch a character from the book.
13. Write a diary detailing the book's events as though you were the main character of the book.
14. Create a cast list and choose who you would pick to portray the cast if you were making a movie version of the book.
15. Make and perform a television or radio commercial to get people to read the book.
16. Cook a meal or dish described in the story, and tell why it was important.
17. Write a story about the characters sometime in the future, after the book has ended. (Did they *really* live happily ever after?)
18. Draw a map of on of the story's settings.
19. If the book has no pictures, design some illustrations for it. If it has pictures, design some new ones in a different style or medium
20. Design a travel brochure to bring visitors to your story's "world."

Suggested Poets

Ages 4 to 8

Lewis Carroll*
Walter de La Mare
Emily Dickinson*
Eugene Field
Henry Wadsworth Longfellow*
Mother Goose**
A. A. Milne
James Whitcombe Riley
Christina Rossetti
Robert Louis Stevenson*
Sara Teasdale

Ages 8 to 10

William Blake*
Robert Browning*
Robert Frost*
Langston Hughes*
Rudyard Kipling*
Edward Lear*
Jack Prelutsky
Shel Silverstein
Alfred, Lord Tennyson*
Edna St. Vincent Millay*
John Greenleaf Whittier*
William Wordsworth*

Ages 10 to 14

Maya Angelou*
Samuel Taylor Coleridge*
John Keats*
Edgar Allen Poe*
Carl Sandburg*
William Shakespeare*
Wallace Stevens*
Walt Whitman*
William Carlos Williams*
William Butler Yeats*

* Denotes the poet has a title in the Poetry for Young People series. Personally, I'm not sure I'd allow my students to read some of these poets at the recommended ages if it were not for the careful selections made by the series' editors.

**Some versions of Mother Goose have been "modernized" – edited to make them more hip and modern. Stick with the old standards, please, if you want to give your children a good foundation in classic poetry.

Literary Math Titles

Lower Level – Younger Children – Ages 4 to 8

12 Ways to Get to 11
100 Days of Cool
Alice in Numberland
Animals on Board
Anno's Hat Tricks
Anno's Magic Seeds
Anno's Mysterious Multiplying Jar
Arthur's Funny Money
A Bargain for Frances
Best of Times
Dear Benjamin Bannaker
Divide and Ride
Each Orange Has Eight Slices
Grandfather Tang's Story
Grape's of Math
Grouchy Ladybug
How Big Is a Foot?
How Big, How Tall How Far Away
How to Get Fabulously Rich
Inch by Inch
I Know an Old Lady Who Swallowed a Pie
If You Made a Million
Jack the Builder
King's Chessboard
King's Commissioners
Leaping Lizards
Less Than Nothing Is Really Something
Math Appeal
Math Curse
Math Fables
Math for All Seasons
Math-terpieces
Millions Of Cats
Missing Mittens
Mouse Count
Number Devil
One Bright Penny
One Hungry Cat
Paper Crane
Patchwork Quilt
Pigs at Odds
Pigs on the Ball
Pizza Math
Ready, Set, Hop!
Roman Numerals
Roman Numerals I to MM
Senefer: A Young Genius in Old Egypt
Sir Cumference series
Spaghetti and Meatballs for All
Tea for Ten
Tikki-Tikki-Tembo
Too Many Cooks
What's Smaller Than a Pygmy Shrew?
What's Your Angle, Pythagoras?
Who Put the Pepper in the Pot?
Zero Is Not Nothing
Zoo Math

Upper Level – Older Children – Ages 8 to 14

Adventures of Penrose the Mathematical Cat
Alice in Wonderland
Archimedes and the Door of Science
Ben Franklin and the Magic Squares
Flatland
Flatterland
G is for Googol
I Hate Mathematics
How to Lie With Charts
How to Lie With Statistics
Jack Tales
Life by the Numbers
Math Curse
Mathematicians Are People, Too
Math Trek
Math Smart Junior
Murderous Math series
Number Devil
Phantom Tollbooth
String, Straightedge and Shadow
Whatever Happened to Penny Candy?

Math Resources

Literary Math Curriculum – Life of Fred series by Dr. Stanley F. Schmidt

Cuisenaire Rod Resource Books:
- Addition and Subtraction with Cuisenaire Rods
- Cuisenaire Rods Alphabet Book
- Everything's Coming Up Fractions with Cuisenaire Rods
- From Here to There with Cuisenaire rods=
- Intermediate Idea Book for Cuisenaire Rods
- Multiplication and Division with Cuisenaire Rod Patterns and Graph Paper
- Primary Idea Book for Cuisenaire Rods
- Using Cuisenaire Rods – A Photo and Text Guide

Pattern Block Resource Books:
- Pattern Block Activities
    - Gr. K – 3
    - Gr. 4 – 6
    - Gr. 6 – 8

Math Activity Sheet

Date:

What I Did for Math Today:

Timeline Page

_____
(Title)

Date(s)

Atlas Quests

1. Name 2 gulfs and the countries that surround them.
2. Name an island in each of the following:
    a. Atlantic Ocean
    b. Pacific Ocean
    c. Mediterranean Sea
    d. Caribbean Sea
    e. Arctic Ocean
    f. Indian Ocean
    g. Great Lakes
3. Name an island territory owned by each of the following in the Caribbean:
    a. US
    b. UK
    c. France
    d. Netherlands
4. Name one major river from each continent.
5. Locate a peninsula (not in the US) and write its name, country and continent.
6. Locate and name an archipelago and the body of water it is in.
7. Name 5 countries crossed by the Equator.
8. Name two seas.
9. Locate and name 5 capital cities in Europe, and their countries.
10. Locate a bay. Write its name and the body of water it is a part of.
11. Trace a continent. Label it and the bodies of water surrounding it.
12. Name a desert on each of the continents.
13. Name an isthmus, its country and continent.
14. Name one mountain range on each continent.
15. Find and name one lake from each continent, and the country it is in.

Science

Topics that should be covered by age 14
- Scientific method
- Types of sciences
- Basic General Biology
    - Cell structures
    - DNA
    - Genes
- Human body
    - Five senses and how they work
    - Basic anatomy and physiology
    - Nutrition
    - Germs and wellness
    - Basic hygiene
    - Basic human development
    - Human reproduction
- Botany
    - Plants – types and their characteristics
    - Seeds – types and their characteristics and development
    - Trees – types and where they are found
    - Flowers – parts of a flower, plant reproduction
    - Leaves – types and their characteristics
    - Photosynthesis
    - Basic needs – food, water, soil, air, sunlight
    - Plant taxonomy – Kingdom, Phylum, etc. and identifying characteristics
    - Habitats/Biomes/Ecosystems and their various plant life
    - Endangered species
- Zoology
    - Animals change and grow as they age
    - Basic needs – food, water, shelter, air
    - Match baby animals to parents
    - Characteristics of different families of animals – reptiles, mammals, fish, birds, amphibians
    - Basic animal anatomy, physiology and reproduction methods

- - Animal Taxonomy – Kingdom, Phylum, Class, etc. and identifying characteristics
  - Habitats/Biomes/Ecosystems and their various wildlife
  - Interactions of animals and plants – food webs, decomposers, consumers, producers, etc.
  - Interactions of animals – predators and prey, populations, migrations, etc.
  - Endangered species
  -
- Earth Science
  - Oceanography
    - Tides, waves and currents
    - Properties of ocean water
    - Ocean floor
    - Layers of the ocean
    - El Nino/La Nina
  - Weather
    - Types of clouds
    - Wind and wind speeds
    - Water cycle
    - Types of precipitation
    - "Extreme" weather – hurricanes, tornados, droughts, etc.
    - Air pressure
    - Weather forecasting
    - Weather patterns
    - Atmospheric layers
  - Astronomy
    - Constellations
    - Sun and other stars
    - Moon and its phases
    - Eclipses
    - Planets and Solar system
    - Space Exploration
  - Geology
    - Rocks and minerals
    - Rock cycle
    - Crystals
    - Earth's layers and tectonic plates

- Earthquakes
- Volcanoes

Physical Science
- Physics
    - Simple machines
    - Friction and gravity
    - Forces and motion
    - Work and transfer of energy
    - Forms of energy
    - Renewable and nonrenewable energies
    - Matter and its stages
    - Volume and mass
    - Physical changes
    - Pressure and changes in matter
    - Density and buoyancy
    - Atoms
    - Sound
        - Waves and how they travel
        - Decibels and Hertz
        - Hearing
        -
    - Light
        - Spectrum and colors
        - Vision
        - Light and dark – shadows, light sources, etc
        - Uses of light
        - Light as energy
    - Magnets
        - Poles
        - Uses
        - Electromagnets
    - Electricity
        - Circuits
        - Batteries
        - Static electricity
        - Currents
        - Charges

- - - Conductors and insulators
  - Chemistry
    - Mixtures vs. solutions
    - Compounds and elements
    - Atoms and molecules
    - Periodic Table
    - Acids and bases
    - Chemical reactions
    - Chemical changes

Scientists
- Edison
- Pasteur
- Da Vinci
- Galileo
- Newton
- Goodall
- Nightingale
- Curie
- Archimedes
- Galen

Artists and Composers

Here's a list pairing artists and composers from similar time periods.

Artists

Renaissance
Giotto
Van Eyck
Botticelli
Leonardo da Vinci
Durer
Raphael
Michelangelo
El Greco
Rubens

Baroque/Post Renaissance
Rembrandt
Linnaeus
Gainsborough
Blake

Neoclassicism
Hokusai
Audubon
Courbet

Composers

Renaissance music – Gregorian chant, English madrigals, chansons, ballads, pavanes, consorts. Henry VIII was considered somewhat of a composer and is often credited with penning "Greensleeves"

Baroque
Corelli
Albinoni
Vivaldi
Telemann
Handel
J.S. Bach

Classical
Haydn
Mozart
Beethoven*

 *Beethoven is often considered the last great Classical composer, and the first great Romantic composer, as he was influential in the transition from one style to the next.

Artists	*Composers*
Romanticism	*Romantic*
Cole	Beethoven*
Church	Rossini
Bierstadt	Schubert
Von Schadow	Berlioz
Constable	Mendelssohn
Goya	Chopin
	Schumann
	Liszt
	Wagner
	Verdi
	Foster
	Bizet
Impressionism/Post Impressionists	*Late Romantic*
Manet	Tchaikovsky
Degas	Dvorak
Morisot	Grieg
Homer	Sousa
Cassatt	Rimsky-Korsakov
Renoir	Puccini
Van Gogh	Debussey
Cezanne	Strauss
Rousseau	Rachmaninoff
Rodin	
Gauguin	
Toulouse-Lautrec	
Seurat	
Russell	

Artists	*Composers*
Expressionists/Cubists/Surrealists	*NeoClassical/Jazz*
Matisse	Bartok
Munch	Stravinsky
Kandinsky	Prokofiev
Mondrian	Copland
Klee	Gershwin
Escher	Bernstein
Picasso	Shostakovich
Chagall	
Dali	
Kahlo	
Klimpt	
Modern Art	*Modern/Contemporary*
Grandma Moses	Miller
Rockwell	Sondheim
O'Keefe	Williams
Wyeth	Webber
Bourke-White	Britten
Pollock	
Warhol	

Please note that these are not set-in-stone divisions. This is here mainly to aid you in planning your artist and composer studies.

About the Author

Suzanne Stewart has been homeschooling since 2002. She attended West Virginia University, and then spent several years teaching preschool and Kindergarten classes in a private school in Columbus, OH before marriage and children. She has been a newspaper columnist, a copywriter for radio advertising, and a professional freelance researcher – making her an official professional Word Nerd. She currently resides with her family, 2 dogs, 4 cats, a fish and a hamster in beautiful rural north-central West Virginia.

Printed in Great Britain
by Amazon.co.uk, Ltd.,
Marston Gate.